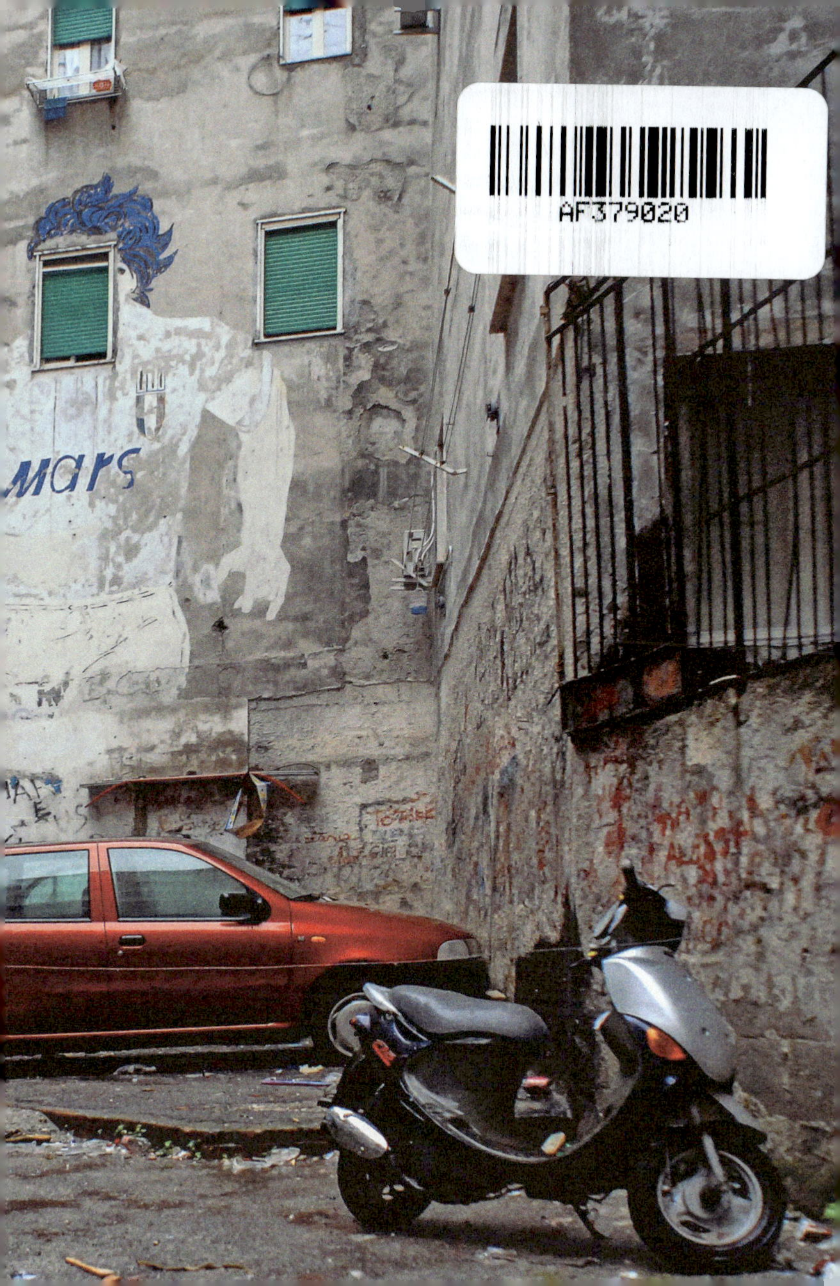
mars
AF379020

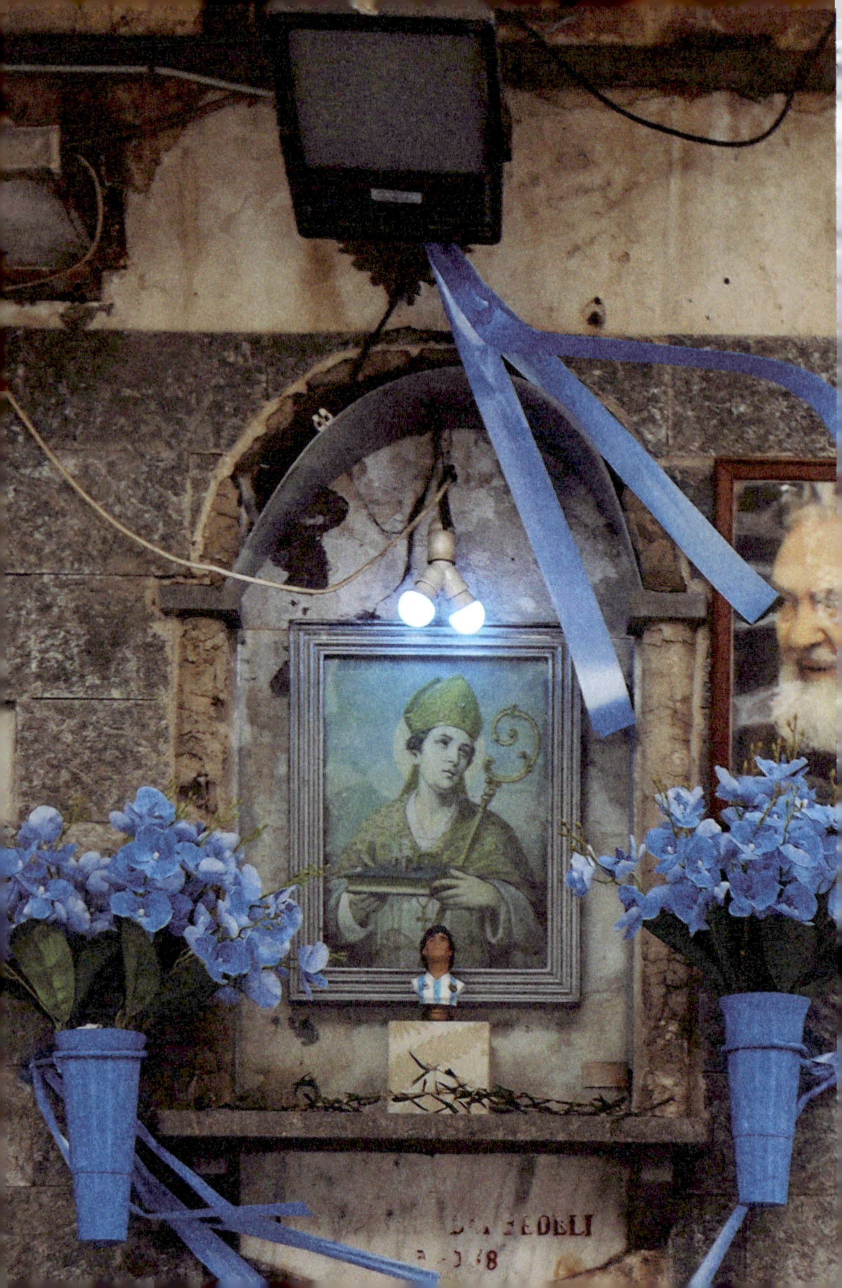

A Directory of Canonisations
around the Turn of the Millennium

David Diehl

ICONS

With contributions by

Mämä Sykora
Andrés David Montenegro Rosero
Alessandro Tione
Asif Kapadia

Edition Patrick Frey

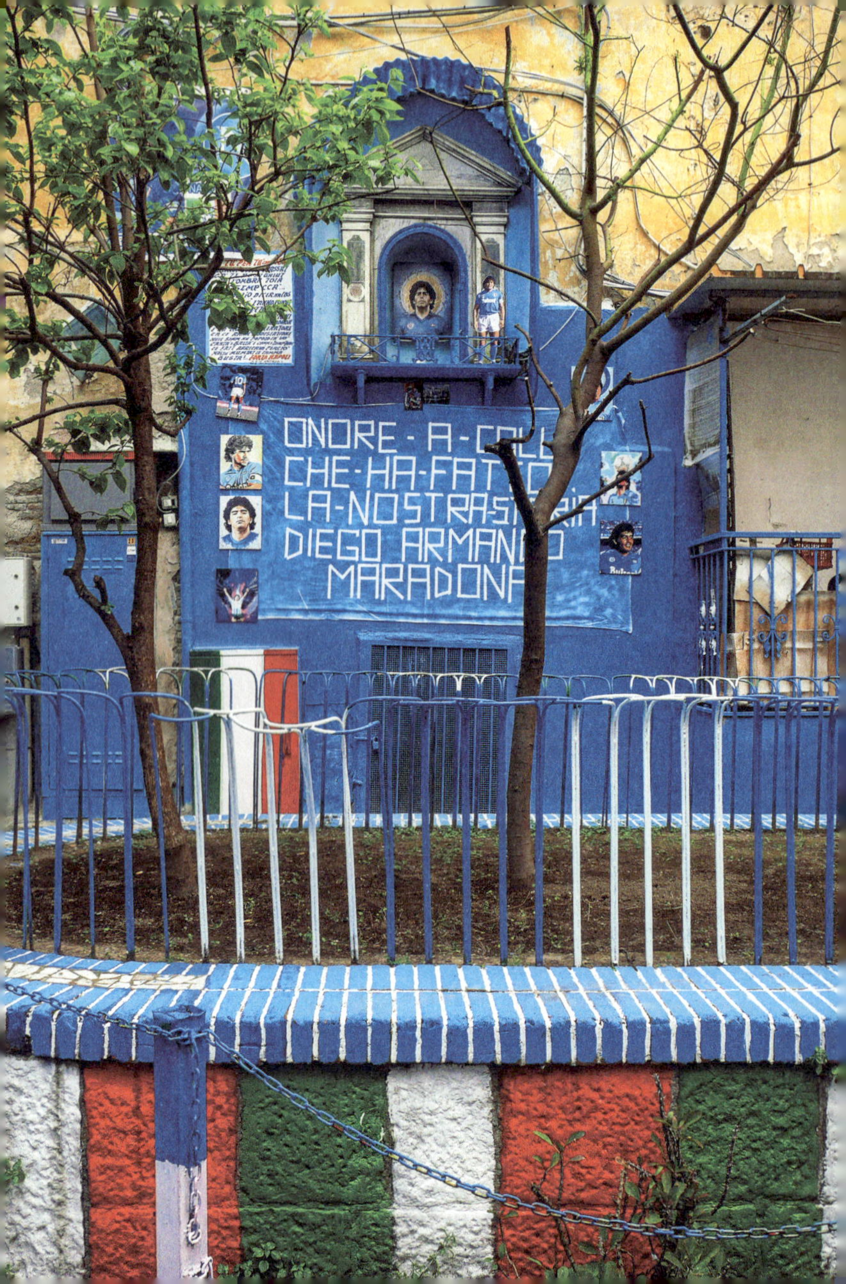

ONORE · A · COLO
CHE · HA · FAT O
LA · NOSTRA · STORIA
DIEGO ARMANDO
MARADONA

This is the story of a picture, one that I painted some years ago. You might think it's just another painting, one among many created in my studio and then promptly ranged in my archives or added to some buyer's collection. But this picture was different in many ways.

It was part of an extensive series that grew out of my collaboration with the Swiss football magazine *Zwölf*. In 2013, after having executed a number of football-related paintings, I was working on an artistic fusion of what are often regarded as kindred pursuits: football and religion. Not in the form of an illustration, much less a caricature—no, in an authentic, earnest style that references Christian iconography, using oils and gold leaf on cedarwood, the way painters worked over five centuries ago. Religious aesthetics, the iconisation of the leading lights of politics, sport and pop culture have interested me—and kept me busy!—for a long time now, ever since I was at art school turning Che Guevara into a rock star and building an altar to Johnny Cash.

So my immersion in the old techniques of icon painting was but a logical extension of this artistic practice. I'd already executed two or three paintings in this form, but it wasn't until I joined forces with Mämä Sykora, the editor-in-chief of *Zwölf*, that it became a commission-based project, in which anyone, anywhere in the world, could order a football icon of their choosing from me, and which took on this subjectivised aspect of transfiguration and veneration. So I'm all the more delighted that now, ten years on, this project is becoming a book. Mämä didn't have to be asked twice to contribute: his homage to the icons takes the form of vignettes that serve not to annotate or explain the paintings, but to provide an added dimension: words that recapture the magic that made these players more than just terrific athletes.

A few years after kicking off in the pages of *Zwölf*, the project really started gaining momentum—thanks to the Internet, of course, which smoothed the way for worldwide publicity and orders placed everywhere from Moscow to Buenos Aires. The magazine ran a piece on the early chapters of this story, including a conversation between Mämä Sykora and me at my studio on Scheuchzerstrasse, during which the project took a new turn. At that very moment, while we were talking, I received a request from a Colombian based in the US. Needless to say, he wanted a portrait of Carlos Valderrama. I momentarily balked at the thought of trying to render all those golden curls: the technical aspects of this assignment would clearly involve a lot of time and effort. But the client's job title under the signature added a promising detail: Dr Andrés David Montenegro Rosero turned out to be an art historian teaching at Bridgewater University in Rhode Island. This was the first time anyone in an art-related profession had manifested a serious interest in my project.

Not only that, but the professor turned out to be a full-blooded *fútbol* aficionado who could recite just about every move ever executed by the Colombian *selección*, including the one Valderrama initiated in that historic match against Germany. It was clear from the get-go that 'El Pibe' would have to be wearing that same iconic red jersey in the portrait. Montenegro was a godsend, embodying everything this project was about for me: a serious interest in art history and an infatuation with football that included—and this was crucial to me—a personal, emotional connection to the subject-matter: ten-year-old Andrés Montenegro had actually attended the match in which the fatal own goal was scored by Andrés Escobar—who, shortly afterwards, was to be the subject of a second icon for my Colombian client. There is more on that story in the pages ahead.

But the subject of the special portrait mentioned in the opening lines of this foreword was someone else. Not Valderrama or Escobar, but Maradona, of course—who else! I painted my Maradona icon in 2017, the forty-second in a series that would eventually grow to seventy-eight icons by 2020. Even as my Maradona was taking shape, I had a hunch it was going to be good. Some paintings just go smoothly, others are a long hard slog. This one practically painted itself. And I knew it would have a special place in the series—if only because it was Maradona, at long last. It wasn't the first picture to show Maradona with a halo around his head. This iconographic attribute was widely used for portraits of him long before mine—and even before the first works in my series. But I felt it gave my painting just the right balance. The halo wasn't a joke or a parody, nor was it a presumptuous conceit. It was the earnest and authentic expression of what Maradona was: not just another footballer, but a public figure whose sheer intensity and spirit of self-sacrifice—as well as uncontrollability on and off the pitch—meant a lot more to a lot of people than just entertainment. He actually *was* an icon. An icon that became part and parcel of Argentine —and, of course, Neapolitan—identity, even in the eyes of ten-year-olds like myself in 1986.

Maradona's relationship to Naples has probably never been explored more deeply than in Asif Kapadia's intense and moving documentary film *Diego Maradona* (2019), the third in his trilogy about stars who became too famous too young, after *Senna* (2010) and *Amy* (2015), for which he won an Oscar. During production, his team contacted me about using my picture, but did not follow up. So when Cord Dueppe from the 11mm football film festival in Berlin sent me a photograph of Asif Kapadia at home with his 11mm prize beside a reproduction of my icon, I seized the moment to get the director's number. I didn't know what I'd do with it yet, but when this book project took off, I did: I wanted to talk to him about Maradona. About his film and my icon, and about the affinity of our artistic approaches of creating new images out of existing material. About Naples. And about the fact that a story isn't complete until people read it and tie it into their own stories and their own references, needs and ideas.

So this is also a story about creating an image and putting it out there in the world, where it takes on a life of its own, roaming and resonating out of control. And then comes home, so to speak, to the place where it really belongs: to Naples. My picture became part of normal life there and part of the nostalgia Neapolitans have felt since their last Scudetto back in 1990, when *their* Diego was still amongst them.

The photographer Alessandro Tione was born here just a few years after Maradona left in disgrace. He grew up on this nostalgia for Napoli's heyday—that's all they ever pined for—as documented in the young photographer's series on manifestations of the Maradona cult all over Naples. They're shot from a born-and-raised Neapolitan's point of view, so they give my painting a new dimension, telling an insider's side of its story as he tracks down reproductions in the day-to-day lives of locals, for whom Diego was, and remains—and this is the very basis of my project—a saint. Coming across the same picture time and again as he meandered through the streets of Avvocata, San Lorenzo and the Quartieri Spagnoli, at some point Alessandro wanted to know who had painted it. That's how our stories intersected.

But we didn't actually meet until much later, at Easter 2023, when this book was already in the works and I decided to pay another visit to Naples to see where else my picture might turn up. In the meantime, for the first time in over thirty years, Napoli finally had another shot at the Scudetto. And Diego was dead—an eventuality that had been the subject of speculation for years, but which came as something of a surprise after all. And it triggered a foreseeable final development: Diego would now definitively become what he'd always been for his devotees— a saint. And what had previously been mooted with tongue pretty firmly in cheek, was now pronounced quite seriously, elevating my icon to a whole new level. That's what the last part of this book is about.

Paintings by David Diehl
Notes by Mämä Sykora

Part I

The game is already lost before kick-off. What's the other side to do about a man who kicks the ball straight up into the sky from the centre circle, so high that pigeons have to dodge it, and then, when it falls, kicks it straight back up along the exact same trajectory? To the beat of the rattling music from the stadium's loudspeakers—and with his laces undone! Psyched out before the match has even started, the opposing team finish their warm-up, don their shirts in the dressing room and brace themselves for defeat. You can't beat God.

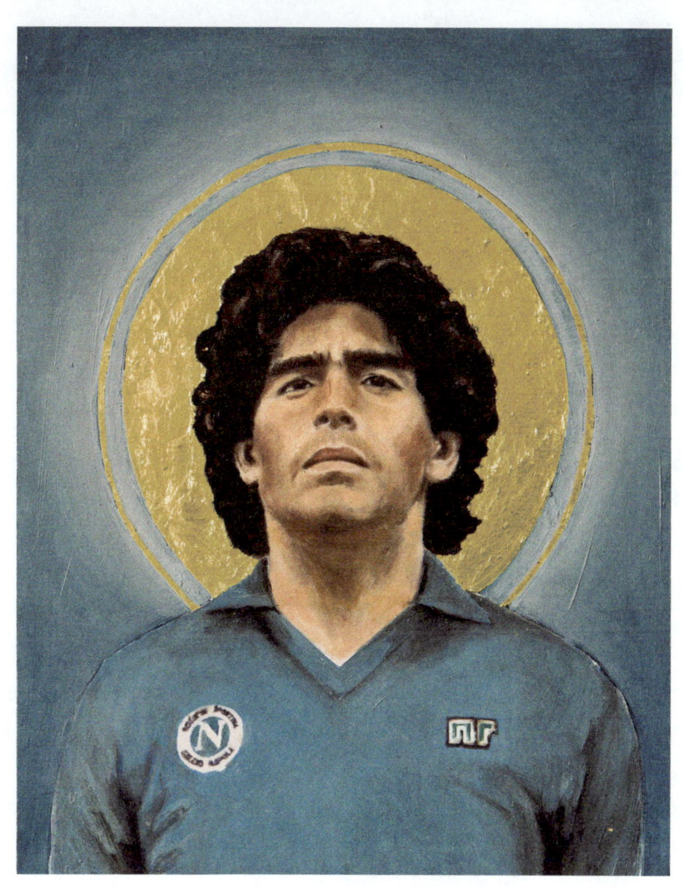

Diego Maradona

He never sprinted, and yet was always first to the ball. He didn't make passes; the ball would willingly execute whatever ideas his foot, preferably his heel, came up with. Standing nearly two metres tall, his body exuded elegance and nonchalance. To him, football was pleasure, and a playful defeat was worth a thousand victories. His game was so captivating that even a traumatic loss could bring tears of joy to the eyes of his fans.

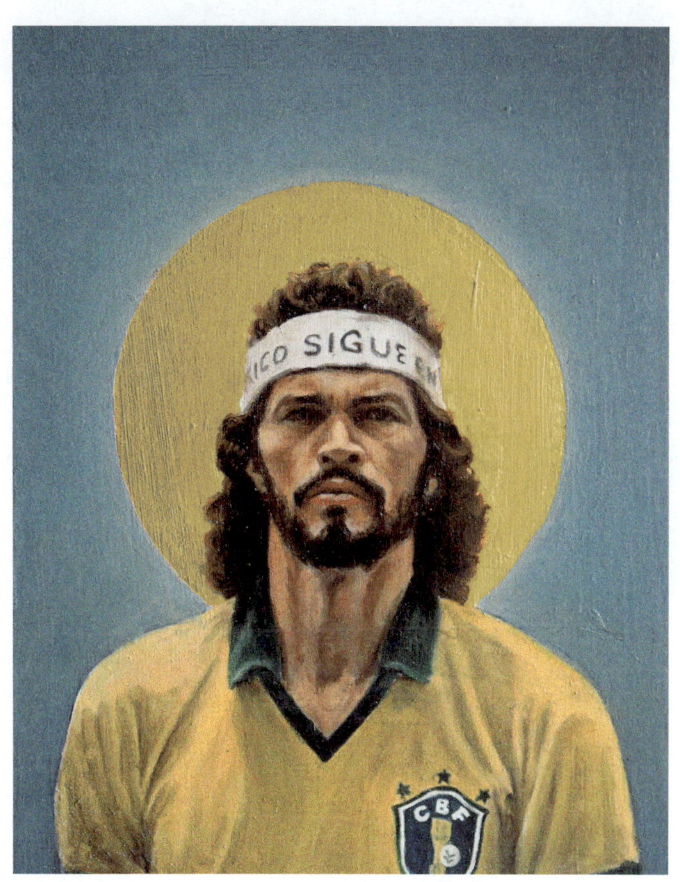

Sócrates

It's all been forgotten. How fleet-footedly he floated across the pitch with his 'divine ponytail' bobbing up and down on his back. How perfectly naturally his passes found his teammates' feet. How his zig-zags lured opponents into no-man's land. But then came that fateful moment when the ball sailed from the penalty spot over the crossbar in a match they'd never have played in the first place without him. He became the man who died on his feet. Along with his whole nation.

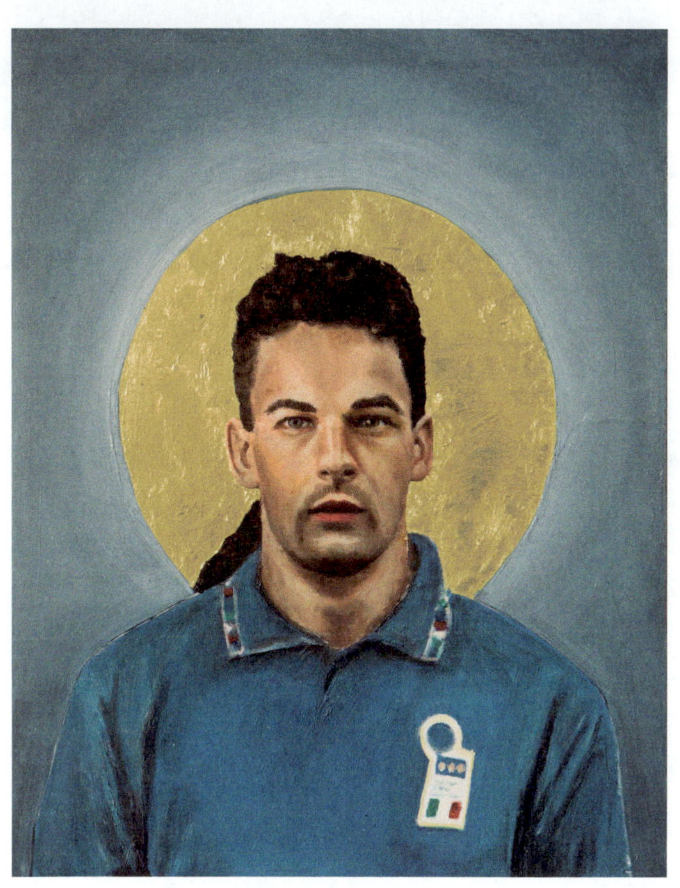

Roberto Baggio

Football had become an old man, stubborn, grumpy, sluggish, till he came along and summarily reinvented the game. Under his coaching, defenders who for decades had done nothing but whack balls and attackers away suddenly became raging whirlwinds. Strikers no longer stood around bored, waiting for scoring opportunities to come to them: they became creators of their own opportunities. And he, in the thick of it all, was all in one, transforming eleven individual combatants into a collective work of kinetic art.

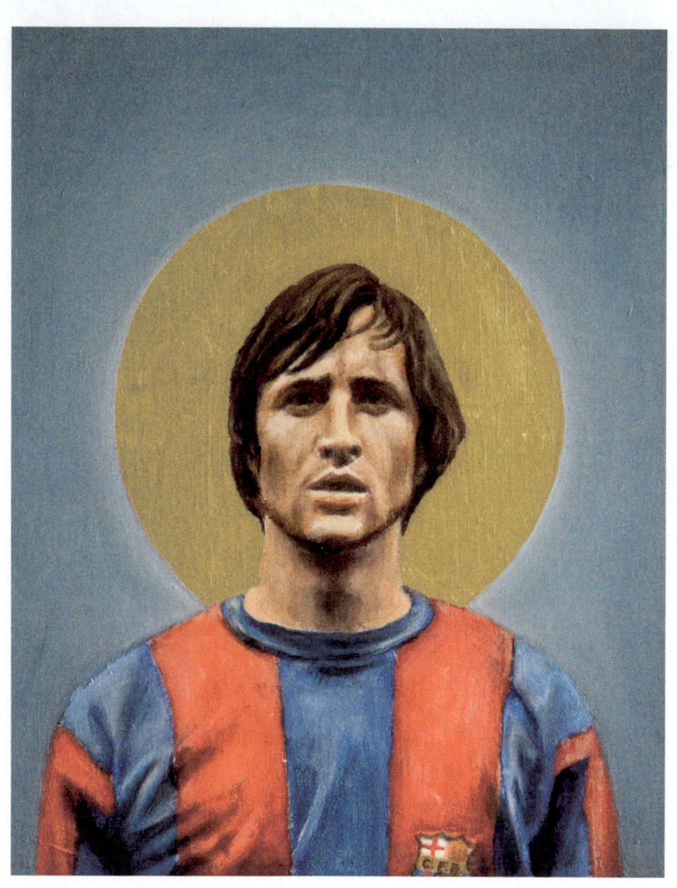

Johan Cruyff

The ball flies back to the penalty line. Suddenly, as if someone had flipped a switch, everything goes into slow motion. Legs spread wide, he stops and waits for the volley: he's the only one who knows what's about to happen. Then he finally swings his left leg, cleaving the air horizontally to drive the ball deep into its home, where even the longest-armed goalkeeper couldn't possibly get at it.

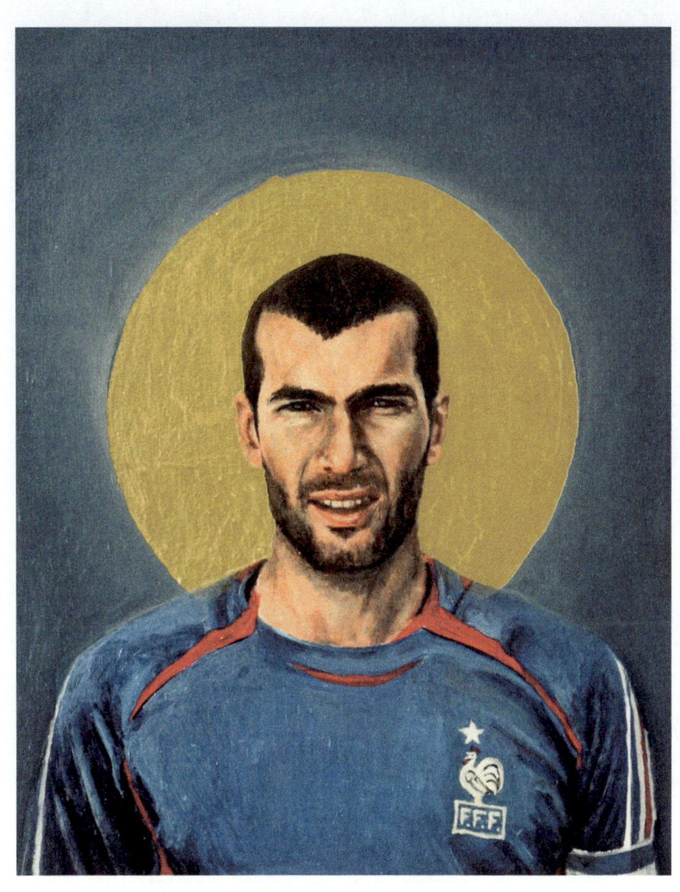

Zinedine Zidane

He's the odd man out on the pitch. While the others are tackling, holding and kicking away at one another, he performs a solitary and enchanting dance with the ball, or takes to the air for a perfectly executed bicycle kick. He's a gazelle among crocodiles, a prince among soldiers, with a sorrowful look in his eye. Because they're all fighting, and he's the only one who wants to play.

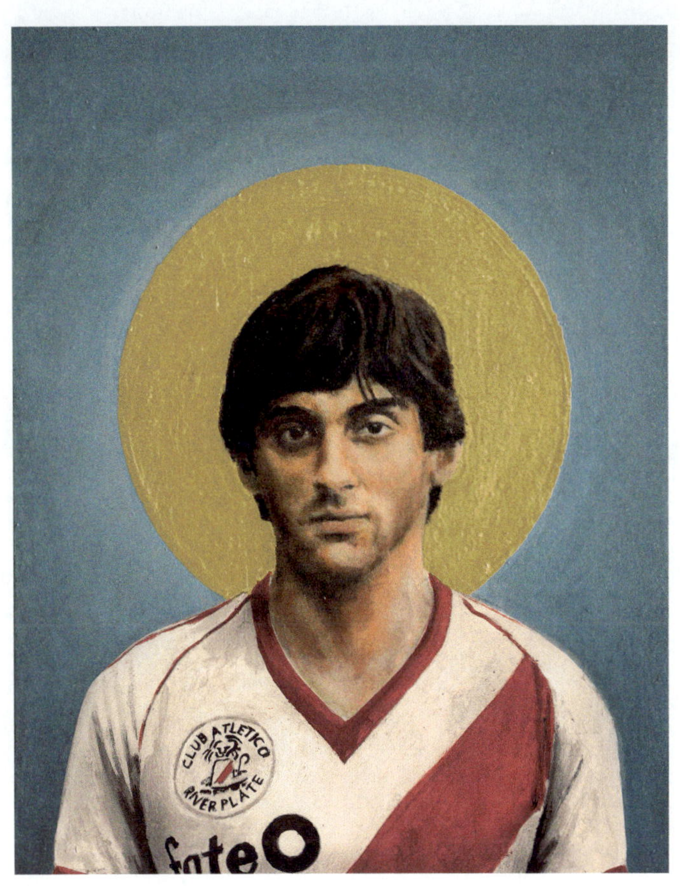

Enzo Francescoli

Tearing wildly down the pitch, he transforms into a beast of prey, his long blond hair into a lion's mane, his eyes fixed on the prize, the ball, from which no one and nothing can keep him. He pounces and strikes the ball, writes Talksport, 'with such controlled violence you'd think he had a vendetta against balls—and nets'.

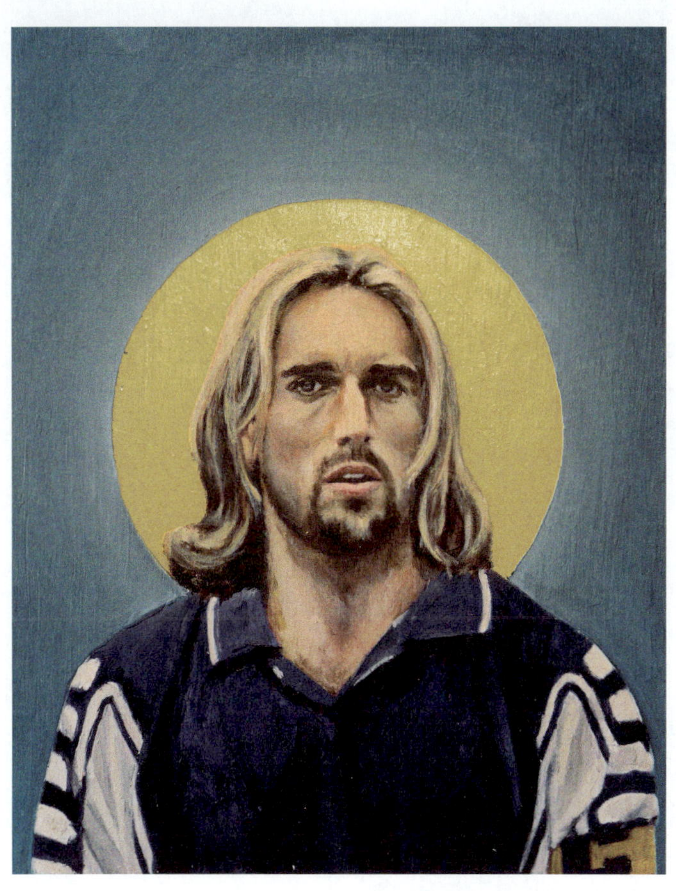

Gabriel Batistuta

The Eternal City had to wait two and half millennia to finally have a king again. And the eighth king ruled not by force, but by pure beauty. When he went into battle, his most potent weapon was the *cucchiaio*, the 'spoon', a chipped shot over his opponents' heads that landed softly behind them. And when he put his *cucchiaio* away, the Eternal City fell back into a sombre slumber from which only a king like him can ever reawaken it.

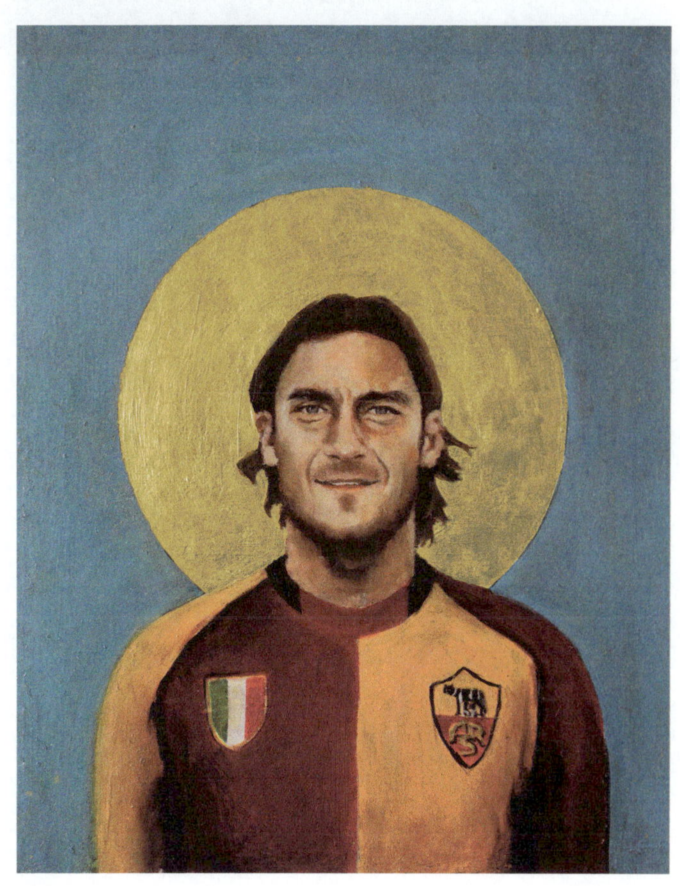

Francesco Totti

When members of his family prick their fingers, the emerging drops of blood spring alternately red and black. Spearheaded by his father, the club had shot up to become the greatest football team on earth. When the number-three shirt was handed down from father to son, the same thing happened. When he quit the pitch after an eternity, it was agreed that no one would ever be worthy of that number again. Who'd have guessed that this dynasty of red and black *gentiluomini* would subsequently live on against all odds?

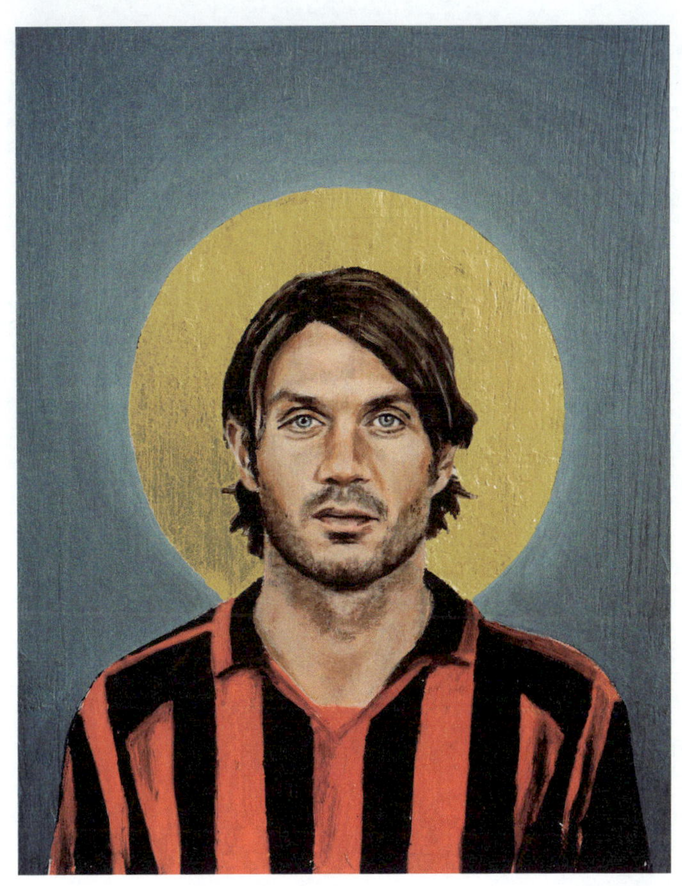

Paolo Maldini

Equally gifted footballers change clubs whenever they get a better offer. Not him. For seven thousand days he stayed on, for seven thousand days he ran up and down the right and left flanks of the pitch, up and down, over and over again. Never tiring, just another little wrinkle etched into his face with each passing year. When, after seven thousand days, he couldn't take any more, blue and black tears flowed far and wide.

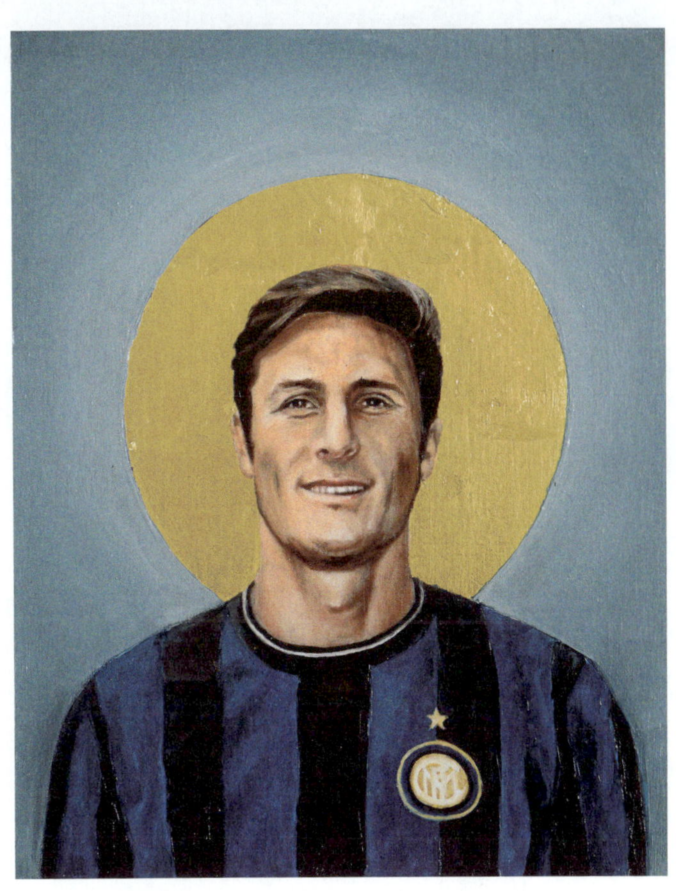

Javier Zanetti

There was no point in arguing with Mamma. So if she said to go in goal, that's what he did. Because he'd perspire less there, and it was way too dangerous out there on the pitch anyway. Which very nearly kept her boy from becoming the man who out there on the pitch would later perform moves of such beauty that they looked like something out of a Renaissance painting.

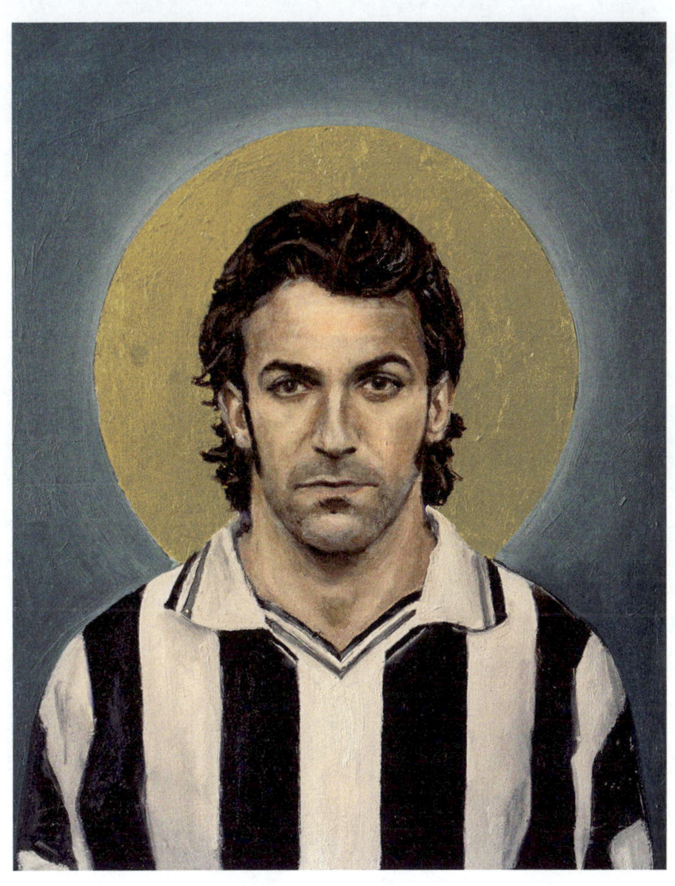

Alessandro Del Piero

The president, a manic millionaire sporting a proud paunch in an unbuttoned shirt, bangs his fist on the table: 'It's over!' Thereby disbanding the entire youth programme of the club at a single blow—the club that the little boy and his whole family love so much. Which leaves him no alternative but with bowed head to go knocking at the door of the hated rivals. The boy rises in the rival ranks to galactic stature, amassing records the way frequent flyers amass bonus miles. Meanwhile, up in heaven, the manic millionaire is still banging his fist on the table. '¡*Maldita sea!*'

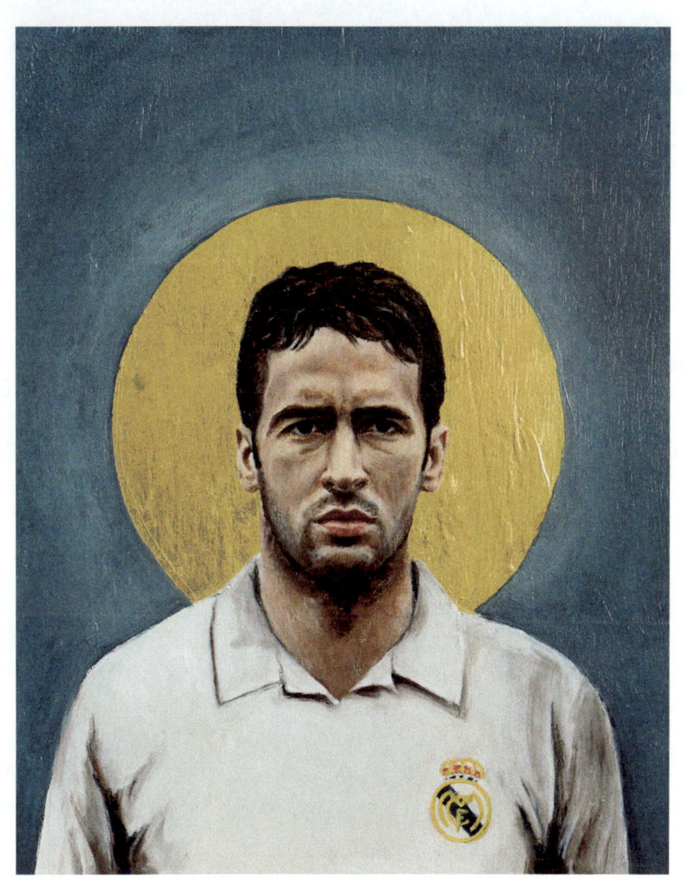

Raúl

The game is an art form, and art should bring joy to people's lives. He played with such artistry that it not only lit up the faces of the spectators in the stadium, but even brought a smile to his own. Like when he'd lob the ball over the heads of opposing players and catch it softly on his boot, or when his feet—did he really have only two?—worked the leather so lightning-fast that defenders were paralysed at the very sight. He smiled, and football smiled with him.

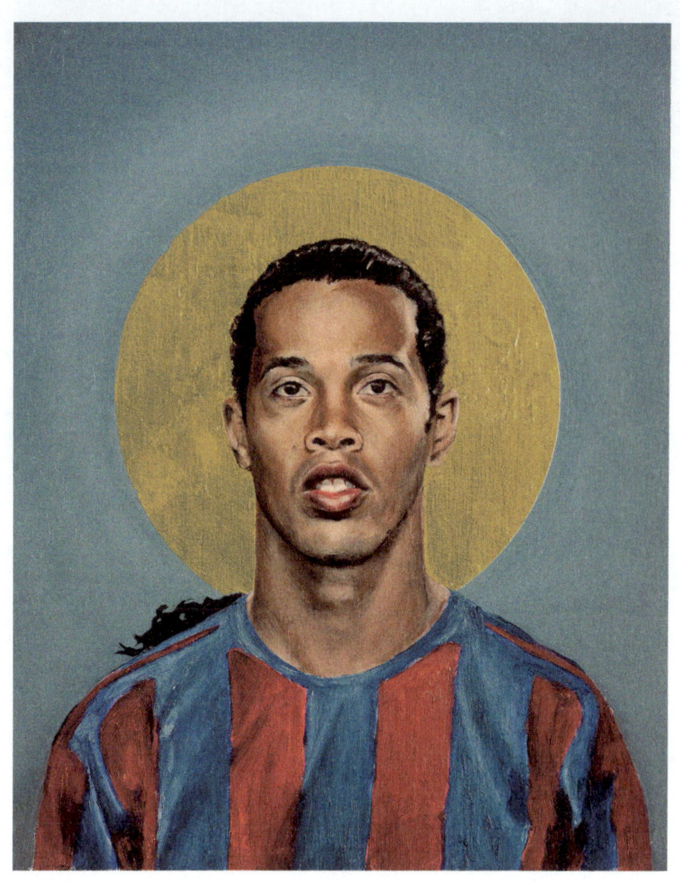

Ronaldinho

Disbelief gave way to despair and, ultimately, panic. The saviour's name was missing from the line-up. Some said he was injured. Others said he was ill, he'd had a seizure, he was on his deathbed. When he did finally reappear, he was but a shadow of his former self, a pale imitation of the man whose supernatural strength and poetic elegance had once called to mind an athlete from the distant future.

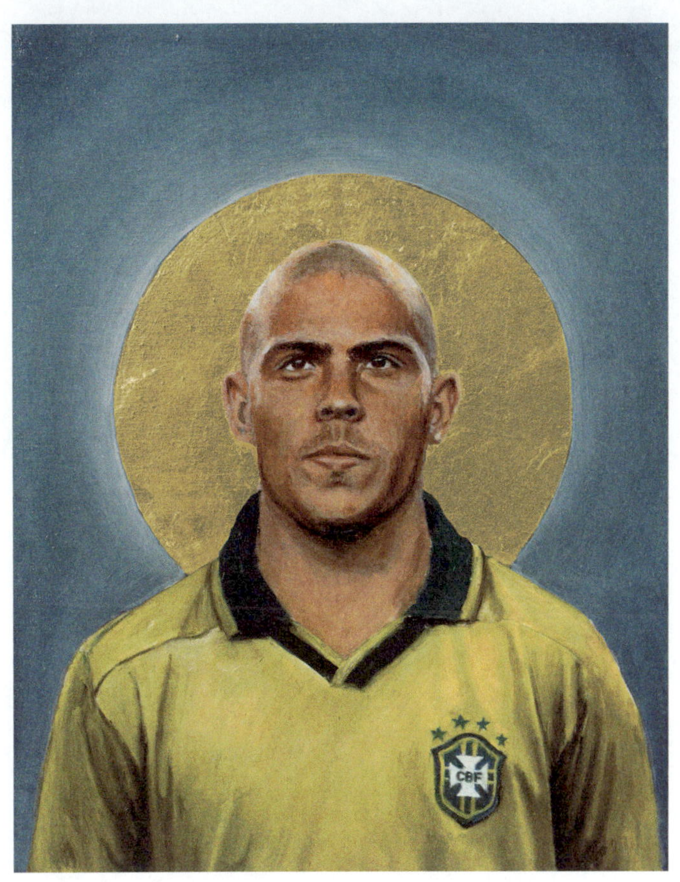

Ronaldo

Although it's raining cats and dogs, a hundred thousand mourners have turned out to pay their respects to the man they'd endowed with the talent of a whole nation. He'd paid them back with spectacle and goals when on the pitch, and with plenty of fodder for local gossip when on a pub crawl. But one day all that talent spilled out into a pint glass in one of those pubs and couldn't be fished out again.

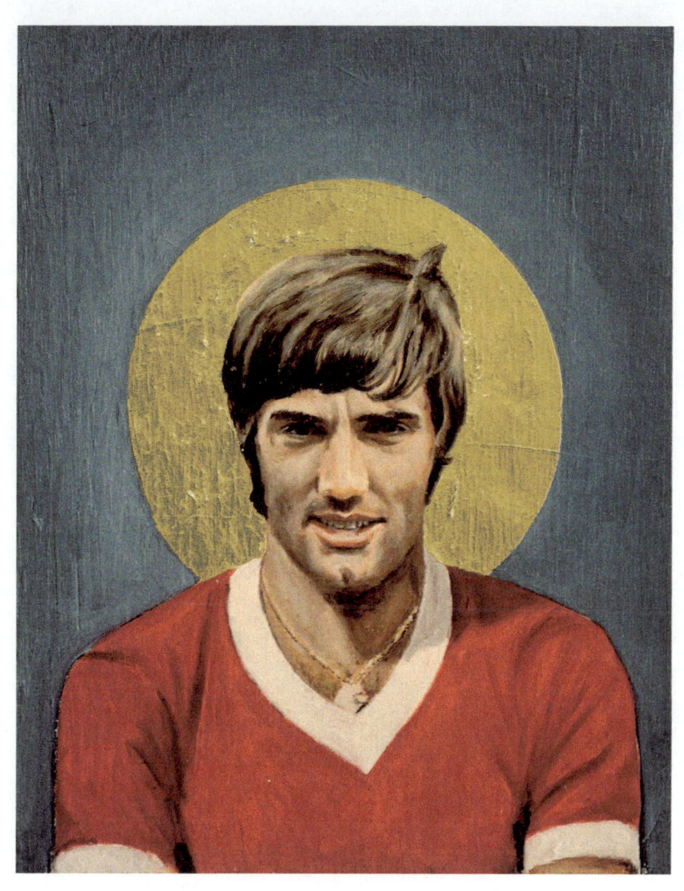

George Best

Many hoped to succeed 'O Rei'. But he was the one
ultimately chosen to wear the number ten: after all,
he'd fought worthily by the King's side in the latter's
final battle. But no sooner had he donned the jersey
than it proved too heavy a load, paralysing him—and
his teammates as well.

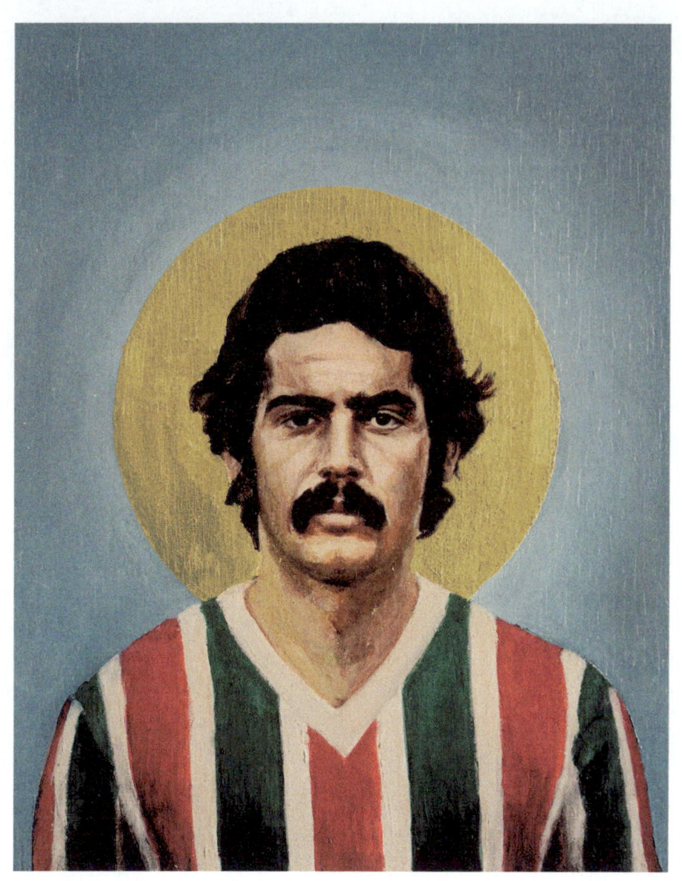

Roberto Rivelino

Thick rain pelts the stadium's thick walls. A thousand cameras and thousands upon thousands of people are waiting in rapt anticipation. He takes a run-up, just a few casual steps, and fires the ball into the bottom right corner. Multitudes flood the pitch, threatening to crush him. But then he resurfaces. Lifted up onto their shoulders, they hand him a new jersey with the number 1000 on it. Church bells ring out throughout the land: the King's thousandth goal, O *Milésimo*, is the holiest of all holy days.

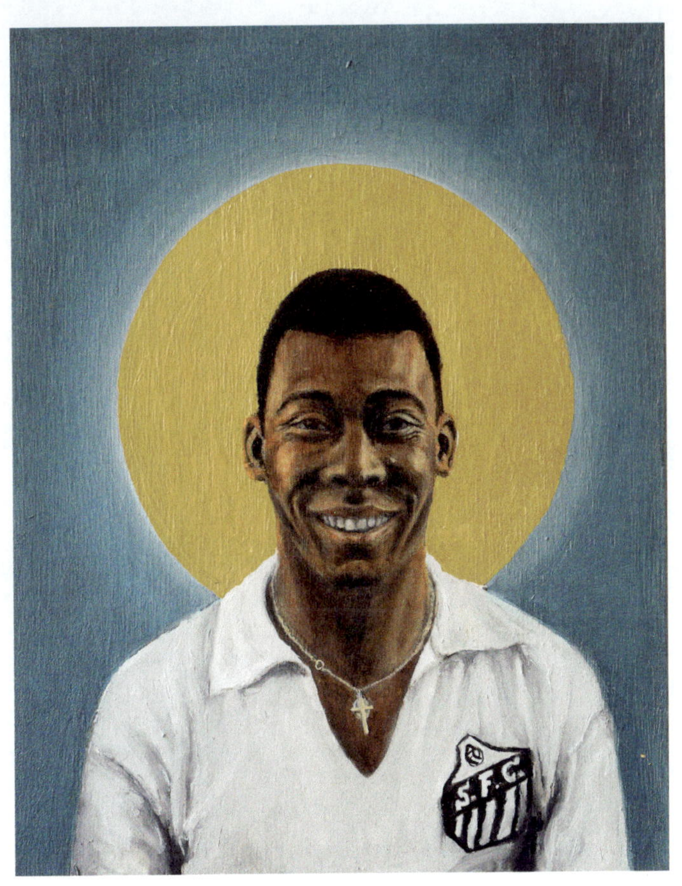

Pelé

He's lying on the pitch, thrashing around, his face contorted with pain. Then he lies still. A whole nation holds its breath. When he's stretchered off, all hope goes with him. But no sooner have the other team scored a goal when he suddenly reappears, frisking around, and makes such an out-of-this-world pass that only his teammate can sense it coming and finds himself all alone, face to face with the goalkeeper. What a miraculous resurrection!

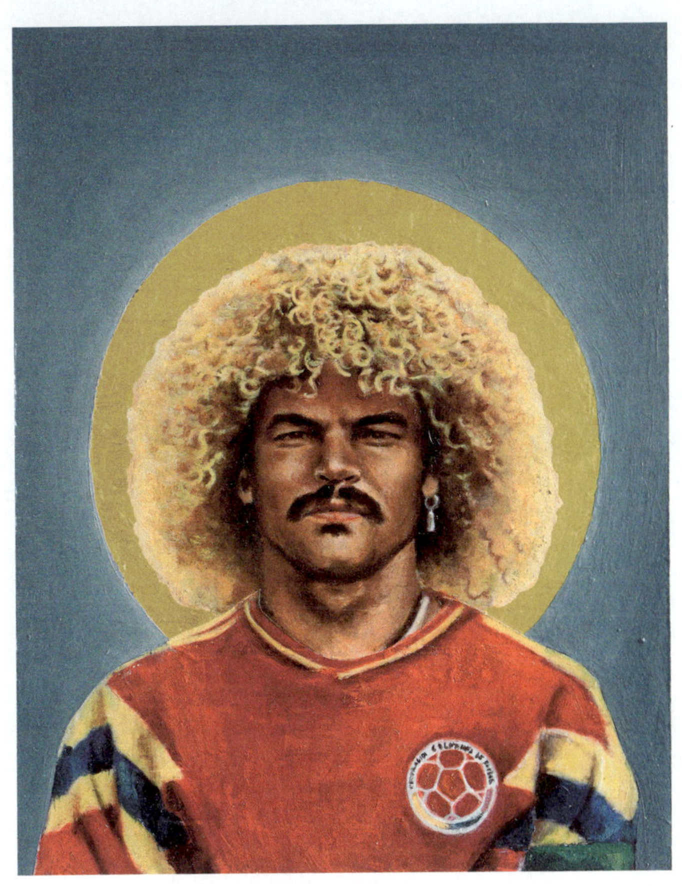

Carlos Valderrama

The soil of Suriname on South America's north-eastern coast is rich in pure talent. And it nourishes the roots of half the *Elftal*, especially those of the 'Black Tulip'. A versatile player straight out of a coach's dream, he's such a multitalent that they don't even know where to put him. When he leaps for the ball, time stands still. His headers are missiles that strike home long before the goalie can even get his hands moving.

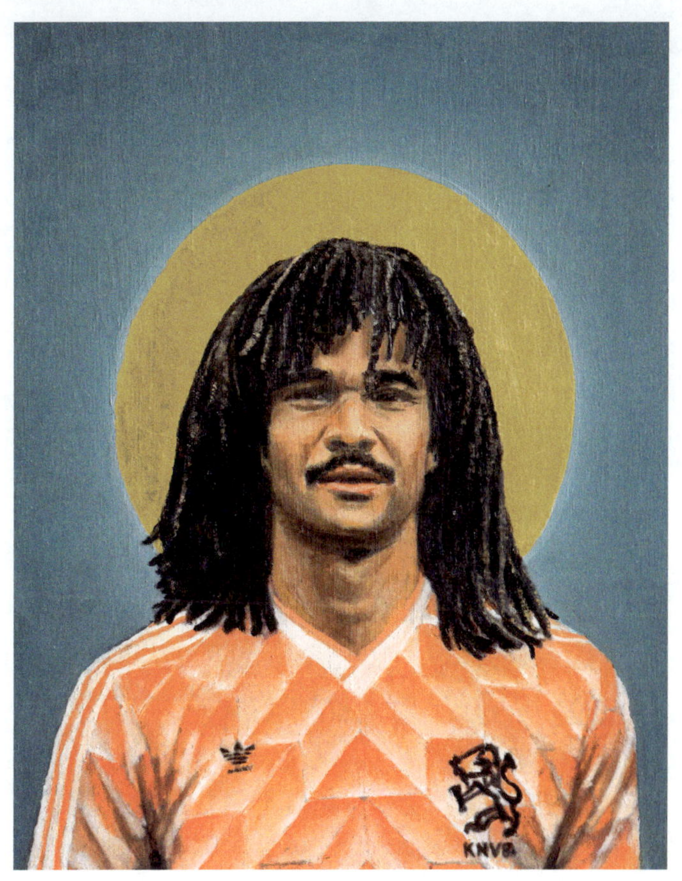

Ruud Gullit

The mother was a Soviet pentathlon champ, the father a cop and a competitive sprinter. The son: a force of nature with tree trunks for thighs. In a race for possession, his opponents looked like promenaders taking a stroll beside—or rather, behind—him. Uncatchable, indefatigable, he charged across the field, the hub of a mighty juggernaut. Everybody wanted him, but he was stuck behind the Iron Curtain—along with his countless trophies.

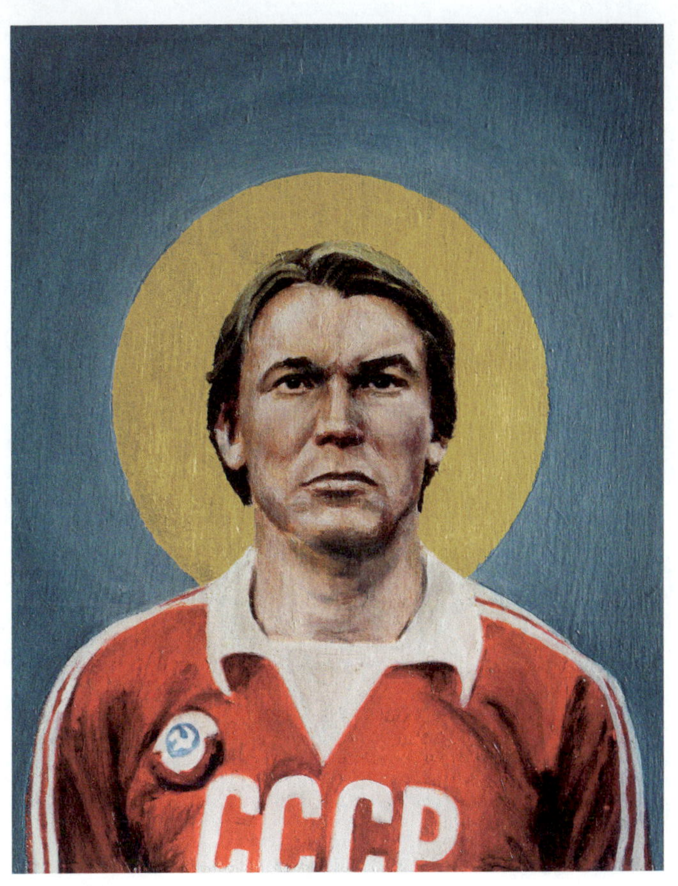

Oleg Blokhin

When a daisy cutter whizzes into the box after thirty-five minutes of play, he's there to stop it: Escobar is just about the most reliable defender around. Which is why the biggest clubs vie for his services. Until that fateful day on which he slides to block and knocks the ball into his own net—and his acclaimed club out of the tournament. 'I'll be back soon,' he writes in a piece for the papers afterwards, 'because life doesn't end here.' But a few days later, he's laid low by six shots outside a bar in Medellín. 'Thanks for the own goal!' shouts the shooter.

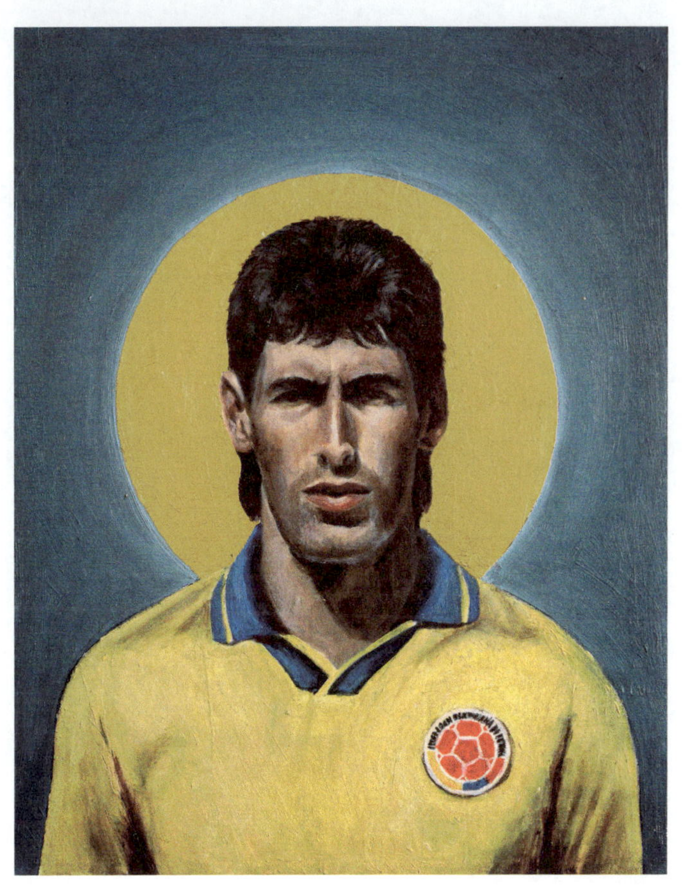

Andrés Escobar

With my Own Eyes

I saw with my own eyes Andrés Escobar score the infamous own goal that would later cost him his life.

I was ten years old when I travelled with my father and maternal grandfather to Pasadena, California from Ipiales, the small Colombian town where I was born, hidden three thousand metres up in the mountains of the Andes on the border with Ecuador.

It was one of the first times I had left my town, let alone my country. We went to the 1994 FIFA World Cup in the USA to witness what was dubbed the best Colombian squad ever to play the game.

We had made it to the tournament after topping Group A of the CONMEBOL South American qualification, sealing our passage to the Finals on 5 September 1993 by beating Argentina five-nil, away from home at the Estadio Monumental in Buenos Aires. Freddy Rincón scored two goals, Tino Asprilla two more, and an eighty-fifth-minute strike from Adolfo 'El Tren' Valencia sealed a magnificent night controlled by Carlos 'El Pibe' Valderrama in midfield. Diego Armando Maradona himself was in the stadium; at the end of the match the cameras caught him applauding the Colombians for their performance. In the aftermath, Pelé publicly endorsed us to win the World Cup over his beloved Brazil. Even Johan Cruyff had our back.

As a nation, we were euphoric. On the way to California, there were streams of Colombian fans all heading in the same direction. You would run into them in the airport, on the plane, at the hotel, walking around host cities. The Colombian diaspora was also present; suddenly I realised that there were

Colombians and second-generation Colombians living in Pasadena, that the national bond extended far beyond any borders—as a young boy, it was incredible to see how *fútbol* activated communities, how it contributed to a sense of belonging even from afar.

The World Cup kicked off on 18 June, and at the Rose Bowl in Pasadena we lost our first game against Romania three-one. Florin Răducioiu had given Romania the lead in the fifteenth minute after wonderful play by Gheorghe Hagi, before Hagi himself scored from long range nineteen minutes later, humiliating our goalkeeper Óscar Córdoba. Just before half-time Valencia got one back for us, but Răducioiu sealed the deal for Romania in the eighty-ninth minute after taking advantage of yet another goalkeeping blunder.

To our travelling group's chagrin, we were staying at the same hotel as the Romanian delegation. After our defeat, I vividly remember waiting for the hotel lift, only to find Hagi and Răducioiu inside when it arrived. My dad really wanted to get their autographs, but I refused to get in.

Our second game was against the hosts, the USA, on 22 June. Kick-off at the Rose Bowl was at 4.30 p.m.; with the mercury at 32.3 degrees Celsius, our seats in a corner of the stadium were in the blazing sun. What made the biggest impression on me was how many local fans were there. Colombians were reduced to a tiny minority of scattered groups surrounded by a very loud ocean of white-starred blue shirts. The USA fans cheered their team on in a slightly different way from what I had experienced elsewhere. They screamed a lot in high-pitched voices; sometimes what they shouted didn't make much sense. To me, it felt as if they were watching a different sport altogether. These were the early days of men's 'soccer', when the USA had everything to play for, and very little to lose.

From my viewpoint, I saw Colombia dominate for long periods of the first half. However, our seats were much closer to Córdoba's goal, so I couldn't really make out or fully understand just how close we had been to going ahead. As a ten-year-old kid, sometimes I couldn't even see the pitch, but I reacted with and through the surrounding group of Colombia fans who could make out the action. For over half an hour we were focused on the opposite end of the pitch. But then, in the thirty-fifth minute, the USA's John Harkes drove through the far side of our right flank and whipped in a low cross aimed at his overlapping teammate, whose run brought him closer to where we were watching on with bated breath. I saw Andrés Escobar slide to block the cross and with his right boot deflect the ball past the hapless Córdoba. Escobar lay back, his head in his hands, as an eruption of joy exploded around our small group. We meanwhile sank into a deep silence. It was as if we had all felt an ominous cloud overshadow the sunny day. We all knew a tragedy had taken place; but we thought it was limited to the match.

We watched the rest of the game as if in a daze—a feeling that was echoed by our players on the pitch, who seemed confused, somewhat disinterested, totally out of sorts. Our defensive midfield had disappeared as the partnership between Hernán 'Carepa' Gaviria and Leonel Álvarez failed to gel. Rincón and Valderrama misplaced several passes and stopped tracking back. Our forward line of Asprilla and Antony 'El Pitufo' de Ávila ambled through the final third of the pitch, but registered only one dangerous shot on target in the first forty-five minutes.

The second half continued just like the first. Colombia took some initiative, but the USA had the chances. Alexi Lalas had a goal chalked off for offside, but in the fifty-second minute Earnie Stewart capped off a brilliant team move by chipping the outrushing Córdoba. We all knew it was over then, and the rest of the half proved us right. The USA had several chances to extend their lead—three or four clear shots on goal. Colombia, on the other hand, only came close to scoring through a weak Valderrama header and a Wilson Pérez shot. It was only in the last minute of regular play that 'El Tren' Valencia managed to put the ball beyond Tony Meola.

Our family photo album of the trip contains only three photos from that day, all captured by my grandfather. The first gives an overall perspective of the stadium and pitch; the second shows the backs of the teams lined up during the singing of the national anthems. The third photo shows my dad and me after the final whistle, sitting on the floor, leaning against a plywood merchandise shack. We both look dejected. My dad is offering me his hand. I remember him saying to me that everything would be okay, that life goes on, that it was only a game of *fútbol* and that *fútbol* always gave you a second chance. Sometimes I think I remember that moment more than the game itself.

I don't remember much of the rest of that World Cup campaign. Colombia won their last game against Switzerland two-nil, but there was a bitter feeling of disappointment shrouding the team's tournament. We went from being favourites to being the first team to return home.

The feeling of bitterness gave way to one of tragedy when we learnt on 2 July that Andrés Escobar had been shot dead in Medellín. According to the official account, on the night of his murder Escobar had been constantly jeered by a small group of patrons at a local bar, who hurled abuse at him for his mistake. Before leaving the establishment, Escobar got into an argument with a couple of individuals who, unbeknownst to him, were mid-ranking lieutenants in a city drug cartel controlled by the Gallón brothers. Feeling disrespected, they ordered their bodyguard Humberto Castro Muñoz to 'deal with the situation'. He did so by emptying his revolver into Escobar as he sat in his car, trying to start it so he could go home.

For Colombia, tragedy now hung over this World Cup. We had known two extreme events in a close period (elimination and death), both interconnected by the very sport that had in the past brought us so much joy. That day, *fútbol* lost one of its rising talents; that day, for a lot of Colombians, *fútbol* died. Escobar became a *fútbol* martyr, sacrificed because of his trade. We were distraught. We were ashamed.

David Diehl's *Icons* series (2013–2020) comprises over seventy portraits of contemporary footballers from across the globe. His moving, verist depictions provide a visual account of the ambivalence of the contemporary football star, caught somewhere between human fragility and divine transfiguration. His paintings use the language of early Christian iconography to comment on the role of footballers, their experiences, and the sociopolitical contexts that surround them. His explicit use of this iconography constructs an image of the contemporary footballer as both martyr and hero.

Despite their mass appeal, most of his works are painted on commission, their starting point individual desires often rooted in personal memories of a specific player, a game, or a feeling towards a cult hero. The final versions are the result of a conversation between artist and patron that imbues the specific portrait with symbolic meaning. His subjects include historical figures like Pelé (Santos), Maradona (Napoli) and George Weah (AC Milan), and contemporary stars such as Lionel Messi (Argentina), Cristiano Ronaldo (Portugal) and Andrea Pirlo (Juventus), among many others. Although originally the series was intended to focus exclusively on male footballers, over recent years Diehl has expanded his works to create representations of pivotal female players including Dzsenifer Marozsán (Germany), Saki Kumagai (Japan) and Megan Rapinoe (USA).

A good example of Diehl's characteristic style can be found in his portrait of Diego Armando Maradona. In popular culture, legendary players have often been described in terms once reserved for divine figures. Maradona for instance is revered across the world as 'D1OS' (a fusion of the Spanish for 'god' and Maradona's shirt number, 10). In Argentina, there is even an official church, the Iglesia Maradoniana, where he is the main saint of devotion. A similar phenomenon takes place in contemporary art where painters, sculptors and installation artists have drawn on the iconography of the divine for their pieces. In Diehl's *Maradona Icon*, painted long before Maradona's death, we see Maradona in the light-blue SSC Napoli shirt worn in the 1989–1990 title-winning season— a fitting tribute to the club that helped him achieve worldwide fame and recognition. In Diehl's painting, Maradona is frozen in time. Although recognisable, his face is also idealised, captured forever at the height of his career. Following the artist's convention, the protagonist's face is perfectly framed by a bright halo of gold leaf that sits atop a blue background. Diehl also includes a secondary halo, a slimmer ring surrounding the main glowing disk located behind the sitter's head. The reason for this slight deviation is to underscore by visual means Maradona's importance to the game—he is, after all, Diehl's favourite football player; he is also considered by many to be the best player in the history of the game, despite Lionel Messi's recent accomplishments.

Maradona's unique character was best expressed by his infamous 'Hand of God' goal, scored using a banned part of the body, the fist, against England in the quarter finals of the 1986 Mexico World Cup. Throughout his career, he was the recipient of two separate fifteen-month-long bans for substance abuse, one for cocaine in 1992 and another for ephedrine, a performance-enhancing drug, in 1994. His personal life was also very turbulent and often played out in front of the lenses of the rabid sports paparazzi. Diehl's Maradona however does not seem to be troubled by any of these personal pecadilloes.

Although all of Diehl's *ICONS* follow the specific template described, there are a few paintings that seem to deviate slightly from his formula. On close inspection of his series, it is noticeable that two of his works break some of the rules. These are the portraits of the Colombian Andrés Escobar and of Germany's creative midfielder Mesut Özil, who played with the German national team until 2018 and retired from the game in 2023. Like the *Escobar Icon*, Özil's painting conforms to most of Diehl's conventions: the frontal three-quarter pose, the halo surrounding the player's face, the abstract blue background. It meticulously represents the last shirt worn by Özil for the national squad, including minute details such as the four stars above the shield that represent Germany's four World Cup victories.

Unlike the great majority of works belonging to this series, this portrait incorporates elongated, slim vertical shadows that emanate from the player's eyes. Diehl allows the colour pigment to run down the face of the player, creating the illusion of running water while simultaneously giving the appearance of a pair of black eyes, the result of some kind of violent attack. They also deliberately echo the religious phenomena of the weeping Madonnas and weeping icons which are popular objects of devotion within Catholic settings. Often, weeping statues, paintings or other inanimate artistic objects are thought to become animate through miraculous intervention. They are often seen as mourning the world as it exists. Often their tears are of blood, as in the famous cases of the Chicago Madonna, the Weeping Madonna of Syracuse and Our Lady of the Turning Eyes in Germany. In Diehl's case, the darkness that surrounds the painting imbues the portrait with a sense of sadness. It depicts someone who has just finished weeping, or who has recently been punched. The main character's right eyebrow is slightly raised, creating an inquisitive look directed straight at us.

This piece was produced in the aftermath of Germany's disastrous 2018 World Cup campaign. Despite being the defending champions, Germany finished bottom of Group F, losing two games (one-nil and two-nil against Mexico and South Korea respectively) and winning only one match (two-one against Sweden). Against all the odds, the team that had dismantled Brazil seven-one at their home stadium four years before was sent home humiliated without even reaching the knockout stage—the first time this had happened since 1938. The German sports press launched a campaign of bitter criticism against the entire squad. Many outlets focused on Özil as an example of the national team's woes. They suggested that he was lazy and out of form, criticised his attitude on and off the pitch, and even openly questioned his love for and commitment to the national team. As a third-generation Turkish-German,

Özil has always tried to maintain his family's cultural and religious connections to their homeland. That is why, in May of that year, he had met with the Turkish president Recep Tayyip Erdoğan to show 'respect to the highest office of [his] family's country'. This short meeting was extremely controversial: Erdoğan's regime had been criticised for human rights abuses as well as being an open antagonist of German interests in the region. Many Germans saw this meeting as a betrayal, as if Özil was rejecting Germany in favour of his Turkish roots. The meeting was even publicly discussed by high-ranking German Football Association executives, laying extra pressure on the shoulders of the already burdened player. According to Özil, 'A German fan told me after a game, "Özil, fuck off you Turkish shit, piss off you Turkish pig."' In other words, the negative feelings expressed towards Özil were fuelled by xenophobic and anti-Muslim sentiments, spurred on by both public prejudice as well as institutional discrimination. As a result of all of this, Özil quit the national team through an open statement released on his social media accounts: 'It is with heavy heart and after much consideration that because of recent events I will no longer be playing for Germany at international level whilst I have this feeling of racism and disrespect. I used to wear the German shirt with such pride and excitement, but now I don't.' His most salient complaint read: 'In the eyes of … supporters, I am German when we win but I am an immigrant when we lose'. Diehl's painting tries to convey these feelings of utter dejection.

When I contacted David Diehl in 2017 to discuss the possibility of creating an *Andrés Escobar Icon* I was overwhelmed by memories. We talked about the shirt he would be wearing, about the expression on his face; we looked at several Panini sticker albums for references, we even traded pixelated video stills to try to find the right haircut, viewpoint, or detail that would add to the portrait. We agreed that the work would follow the rules and logic established by the series dedicated to greats of the beautiful game across many generations, nations and clubs. The *Escobar Icon* would, like the rest of the *Icons*, be painted in oil on pine, in the artistic tradition of icon paintings anchored in the visual language of the Byzantine and early Christian periods. Like most Byzantine and early Christian icons privately commissioned, Diehl's works are also small, measuring 28 by 35 centimetres. Their size and extreme verisimilitude encourages careful looking, creating a sense of intimacy and individual contemplation. This ethereal setting creates a visual homage to Giotto's frescoes in the Scrovegni Chapel, an artistic tour de force created at the crossroads of the Byzantine and early Christian aesthetics. As in Giotto's murals, each of Diehl's subjects is surrounded by a golden halo that frames and spotlights the face while also making the protagonist stand out from their surroundings. Diehl's works follow a formula defined by frontal positions, golden halos, and nondescript backgrounds that create works that are both portraits and memorials of characters.

Diehl's *Escobar* painting expresses his characteristic style. In the work we see Escobar wearing the

yellow Colombia shirt worn at the 1994 World Cup—
a fitting nod to the tournament that cost him his
life. The shirt is recognisable by its design, and by
the inclusion of the Colombia National Football Federation's crest. The work cuts Escobar's body right
under the chest, almost matching the length of a
standard football shirt. The *Escobar Icon*, however,
also represents a slight deviation from Diehl's usual
formula. Out of all of Diehl's works, Escobar's is the
only one that has a prominent, dark shadow cover-
ing almost a third of the sitter's face and neck. This
ominous presence points to Escobar's awful fate.

Almost thirty years have passed since Escobar's own
goal and subsequent death. In these three decades
many details have emerged about the turmoil inside
Colombia's camp during USA '94. Several players and
staff members have given their first-hand account of
a series of key moments that 'sabotaged' Colombia's
performance in the tournament. According to them,
problems started before the World Cup itself. In 1993
René 'El Loco' Higuita—Colombia's star goalkeeper—was sentenced to jail for acting as an interme-
diary in negotiations to free a victim of a kidnapping
undertaken by the drug kingpin Pablo Escobar in
their hometown of Medellín. Higuita's personal relationship with Escobar had been established many
years earlier. As part of his efforts to 'give back' to his
community, Escobar built several football pitches in
the impoverished neighbourhoods surrounding the
city. Higuita, as well as many other Colombian players participating in USA '94, such as Luis 'Chonto'

Herrera, Mauricio 'Chicho' Serna, Hernán Gaviria and Gabriel 'Barrabas' Gómez, grew up playing on those pitches. Higuita's ties to Escobar, along with his indefinite jail sentence, cost him a spot in the famous five-nil victory against Argentina as well as preventing him from making Colombia's World Cup squad.

Higuita's replacement, Óscar Córdoba, has expressed his bemusement at Colombia's preparation for that tournament. In an interview published in Mauricio Silva Guzmán's book *El 5-0* (2013), Córdoba confesses that the team never saw any tactical analysis of their rivals, nor did they watch videos focusing on their strengths or weaknesses. He mentions that the first time that he saw a video of Hagi striking the ball from long range was in a journalist's hotel room the night before the game against Romania. 'After seeing that I got worried, but it was already too late to react. The truth is we did not know them as a team and our sin was to think that we were better. Our overwhelming sense of being the favourites was accompanied by an equal dose of inexperience.' In the same interview, Córdoba also complains that, while Colombia did not undertake any video or tactical research on opponents, both Romania and the USA had scouts present at many of the preparatory games played by Colombia in the run-up to the World Cup. In one particularly illuminating passage, Córdoba narrates how at almost every stage of their preparation for the World Cup there was a *gringo* from the USA present, taking furious notes during Colombia's training and friendly games.

But perhaps one of the most destabilising series of events took place in the days between matches, after the loss to Romania and before kick-off against the USA. As narrated by 'Chonto' Herrera in the ESPN documentary *The Two Escobars* (2010), 'After the loss to Romania, everyone was waiting for me in the hotel. Coach told me my father called. My brother had been killed in Medellín.' Speculation ran rampant. Some in Colombia thought that underground betting gangs—controlled by the nation's top drug lords—were involved. Others argued that it was an accidental death. Regardless, Herrera wanted to leave the camp and return to Colombia to be with his family during a difficult time. Andrés Escobar convinced him to stay by underscoring that they were representing an entire nation, and that the best tribute he could give to his brother was to play through his pain. A sense of fear mixed with expectation seems to have taken over the *selección* from that point on.

On match day, all the players were gathered together waiting for their manager, Francisco 'Pacho' Maturana, and his assistant, Hernán Darío 'El Bolillo' Gómez. According to Asprilla, the hotel meeting room was quiet, and the players were obviously tense and filled with expectation as they waited for their tactical instructions. However, according to Leonel Álvarez, the coaching staff were nowhere to be found. About half an hour later than agreed, Maturana finally showed up. He was visibly shaken and had tears running down his cheeks. He told the team that he had received several death threats and that the entire team had been targeted. In *The Two Escobars*, Asprilla recounts how he went up to his room immediately after hearing from Maturana and turned on his TV. Displayed on the screen were a series of death threats that demanded that 'Barrabas' Gómez be left out of the starting eleven. If not, everyone involved with the Colombian World Cup tournament —players and staff alike—would be in danger. As a result, Maturana decided not to play Gómez against the USA, replacing him with 'Carepa' Gaviria in spite of his conviction that he needed to play the same team that had lost against Romania. With bitter sadness, Maturana said of this incident: 'They won. They beat me this time. And so, I pulled "Barrabas".' Gómez retired from football immediately after learning that he would not play against the World Cup hosts.

Given all of these factors, it is not surprising that the Colombian team melted in the heat of the California sun. Maturana had made two important substitutions: Gaviria for Gómez and De Ávila for Valencia. Valencia was flying at Bayern Munich while De Ávila was the starting attacker for América de Cali (a club owned by another Colombian gang, the Cali Cartel). The key midfield quartet that had brought Colombia so much joy did not feature (Álvarez, 'Barrabas', Rincon, Valderama) and so the team looked confused, haphazard, disorganised. The few chances that were created could not be finished: Asprilla was having a terrible afternoon. The prelude to Escobar's own goal summed it up: Colombia failed to build up play from the back, lost the ball right in the middle of the pitch, were incapable of stifling the counter-attack, before the defensive midfielder, Gaviria, and right-back, Wilson Pérez, allowed Harkes to cross the ball. The team was broken both tactically and psychologically.

At a time when many Colombian footballers were known for extravagant displays of wealth and for befriending dubious characters within the Colombian landscape, Andrés Escobar never caused a scandal and lived a very humble life. He also had an impeccable career as a central defender and was known for clean tackles that relied on timing over physical strength. He was nicknamed 'El Caballero' (The Gentleman) for his graciousness and gentleness on and off the ball. As his fiancée at the time, Pamela Cascardo, declared, he was about to sign a deal with the mighty AC Milan—he was the first Colombian player to ever receive such an offer from the *Rossoneri*. He had his whole life ahead of him, trophies to fight for, other defeats to endure. In the aftermath of the '94 debacle, he insisted on returning to Colombia to 'face the people', to be held accountable, to take responsibility for his mistake and become stronger. To move on.

According to Escobar's brother Santiago, when Andrés returned to Medellín he felt uplifted and supported by the Colombian people. Within a few days of arriving back home he returned to his favourite bars and restaurants. He let his guard down and decided to lead a normal life. 'Chonto' Herrera remembers turning down a few invitations from Escobar; Maturana remembers telling him: 'Be very careful;

the streets are dangerous. And you know that in Colombia conflicts aren't solved with fists.'

Upon his return, Escobar wrote a column for *El
Tiempo*, the nation's biggest newspaper. Published
on 29 June, in it he took responsibility for his mistake, thanked the fans and his teammates, and em-
phasised that one must have the same 'gallantry' in
victory as in defeat. He argued that the team had
lacked *verraquera*—Colombian slang for 'guts'—to
overcome the difficult moments that they faced in
each game. He remarked that both the USA and
Romania had won because they had more 'faith' in
themselves and their ability to get a result, and that
Colombia had rushed and not kept possession or
control of the matches. He pleaded with the nation
to look forward, to trust the process led by the Colombian Federation and to support each other. He
closed his address by saying: 'See you soon, because
life does not end here.' Just a few days later he was
dead.

Diehl's *Escobar* painting mournfully memorialises its
subject matter; it recognises and brings to light the
darkness behind his passing; it is a tribute to the
dead based on the memory of those who are living.
It activates several layers of memory; even though it
is a recent artwork it feels as if it is covered by the
patina of time. When we see Diehl's *Escobar*, we are
not only mourning the loss of Andrés the person, his
future, his dreams. We are also mourning that '94
team itself, a generation that fell victim to its own
success. After the World Cup, the Colombian press

showed no mercy to players or staff, often publishing vitriolic articles decrying the failure and humiliation we had experienced as a nation. To say that that generation was metaphorically crucified in public for their mistakes would not be an exaggeration. Diehl's *Escobar Icon* perfectly demonstrates how an artwork can activate several historical dimensions at once. It is a space–time vortex. A tunnel that all at once transports us to Byzantium, to Pasadena, to Medellín.

Photographs by Alessandro Tione

Religione Monoteistica

In search of Diego. Alessandro Tione compiles
a visual archive, capturing
Maradona's essence in the streets of Naples,
his hometown.

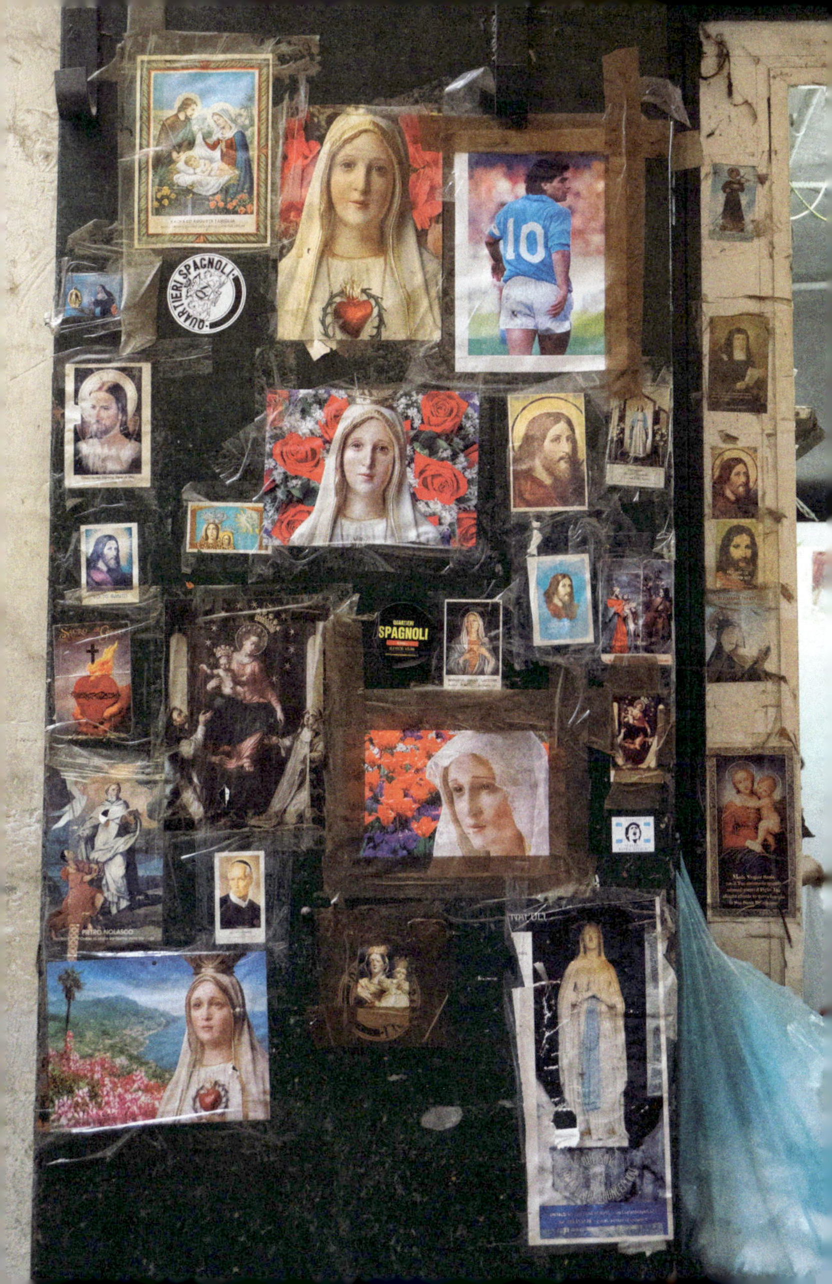
QUARTIERI SPAGNOLI
10
QUARTIERI SPAGNOLI
PIETRO NOLASCO

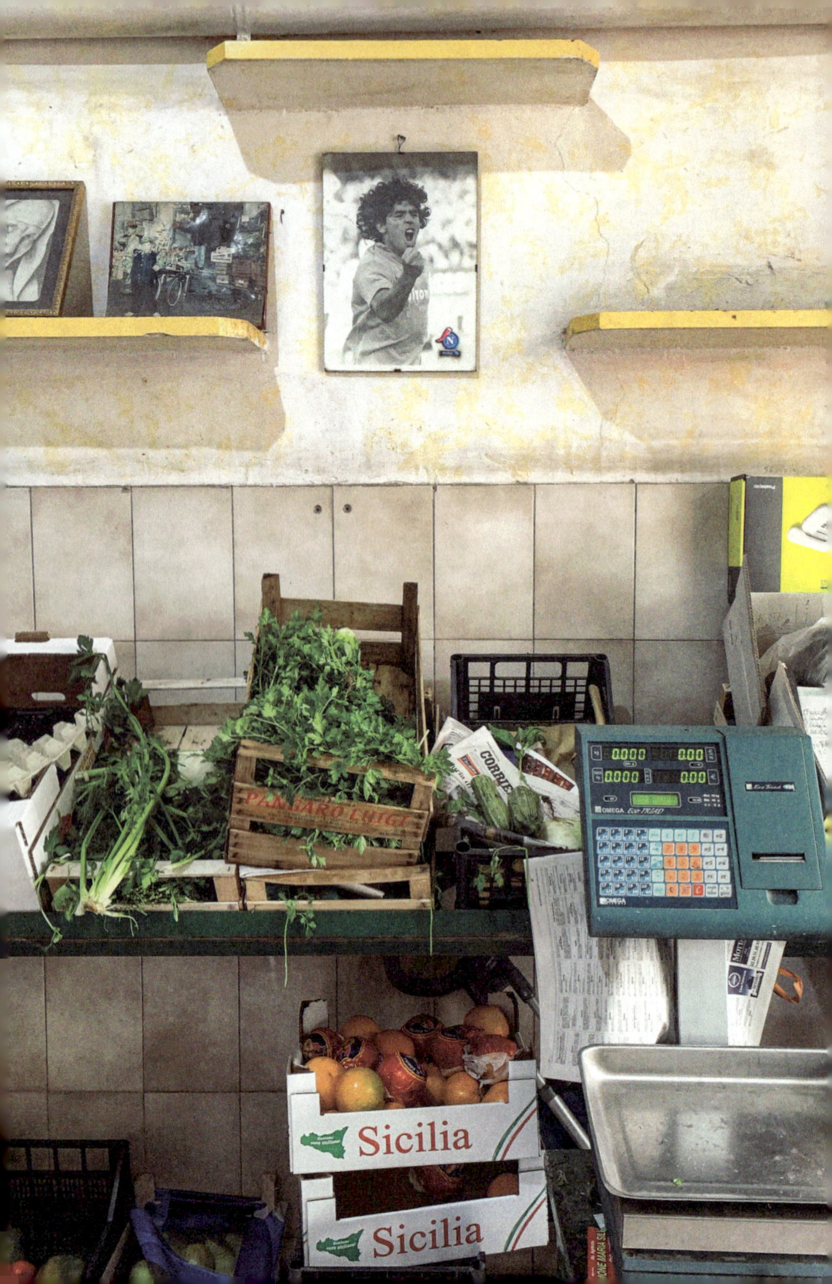
PANGARO LUIGI
CORRIE
OMEGA Eco TRIAD
Sicilia
Sicilia

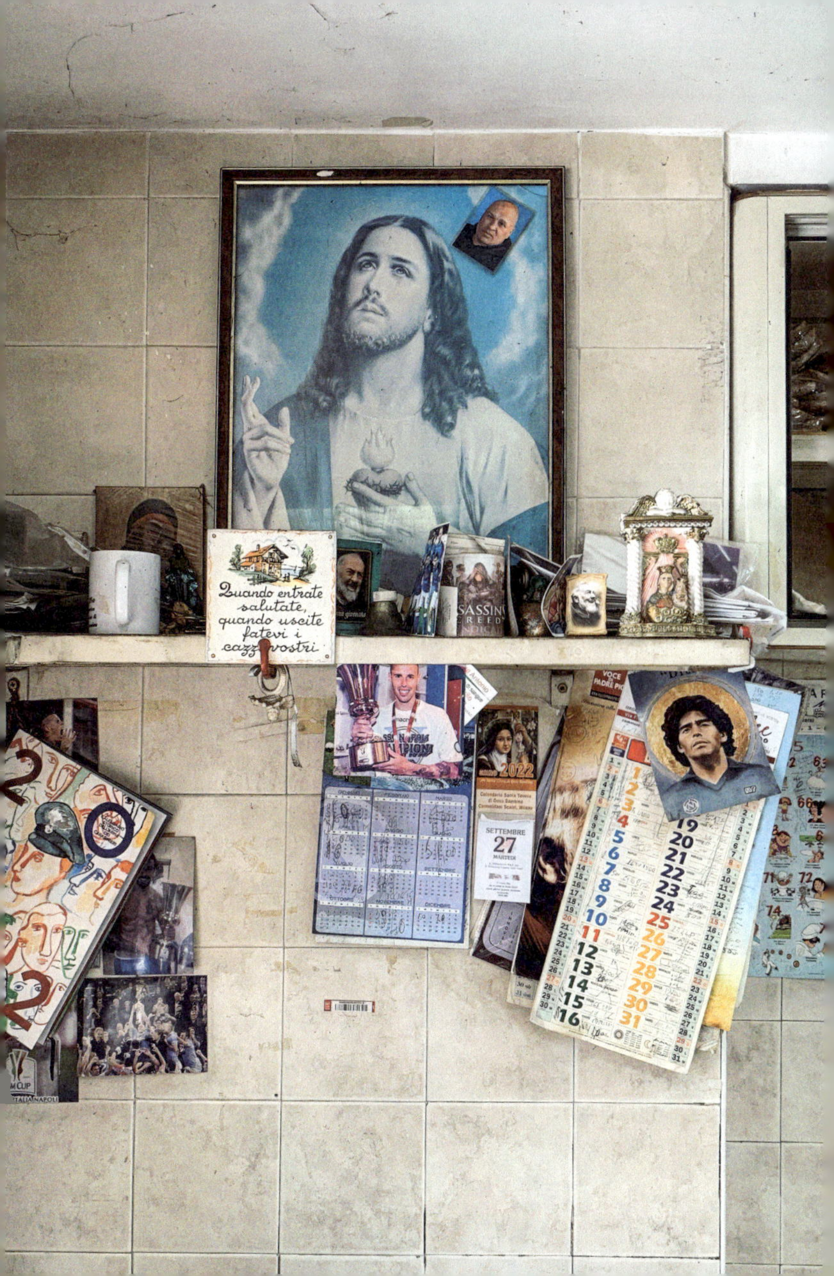
Quando entrate
salutate,
quando uscite
fatevi i
cazzi vostri

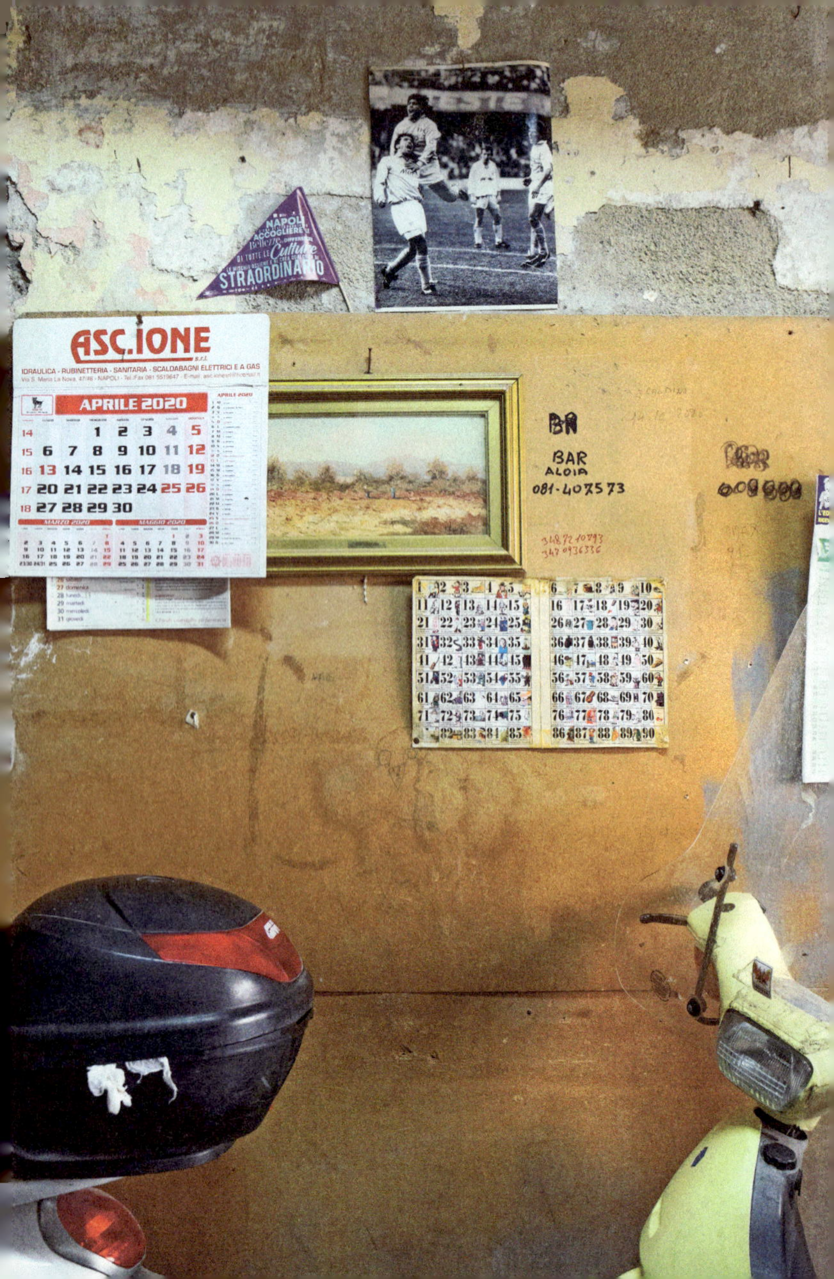

STRAORDINARIO
ASC.IONE
IDRAULICA - RUBINETTERIA - SANITARIA - SCALDABAGNI ELETTRICI E A GAS
APRILE 2020
BN
BAR
ALOIA
081-407573

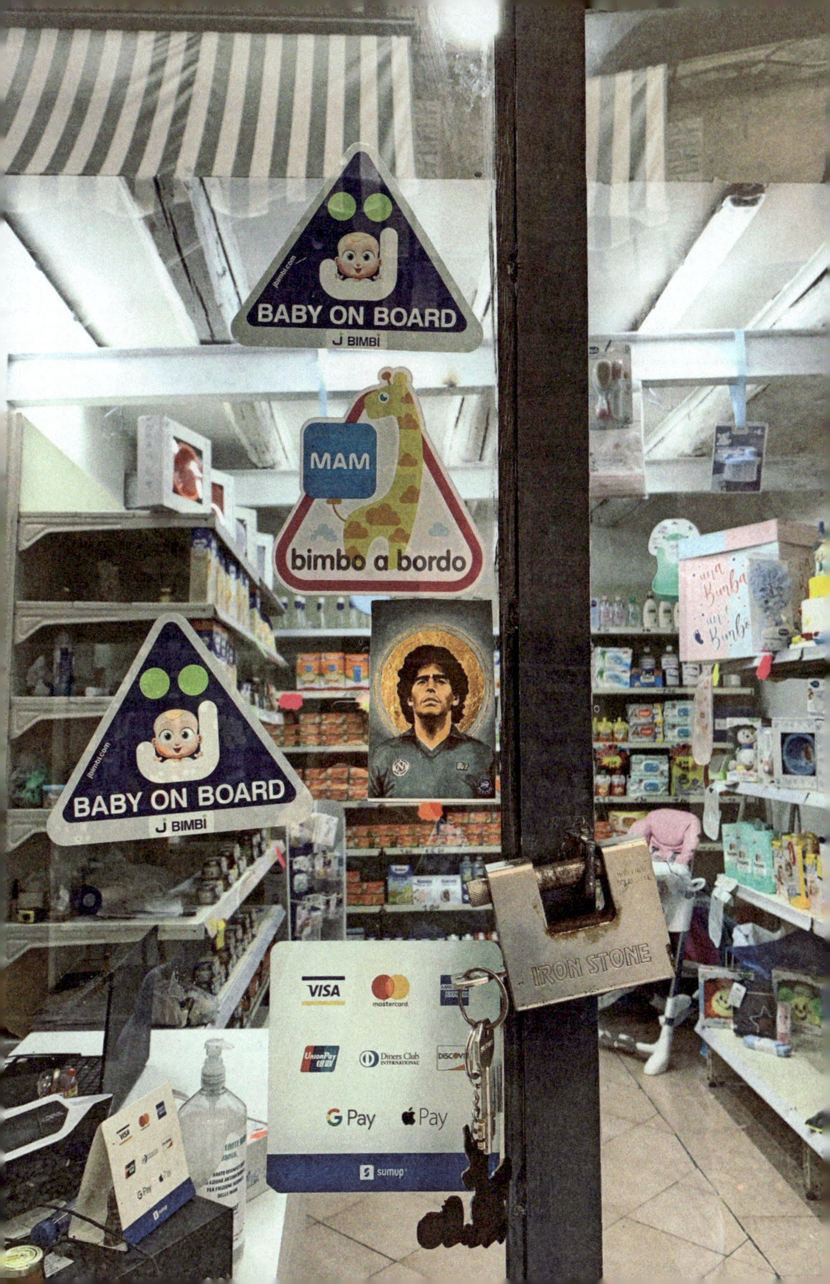
jbimbi.com
BABY ON BOARD
J BIMBI
MAM
bimbo a bordo
jbimbi.com
BABY ON BOARD
J BIMBI
IRON STONE
VISA
mastercard
AMEX
UnionPay
Diners Club INTERNATIONAL
DISCOVER
G Pay
Pay
sumup

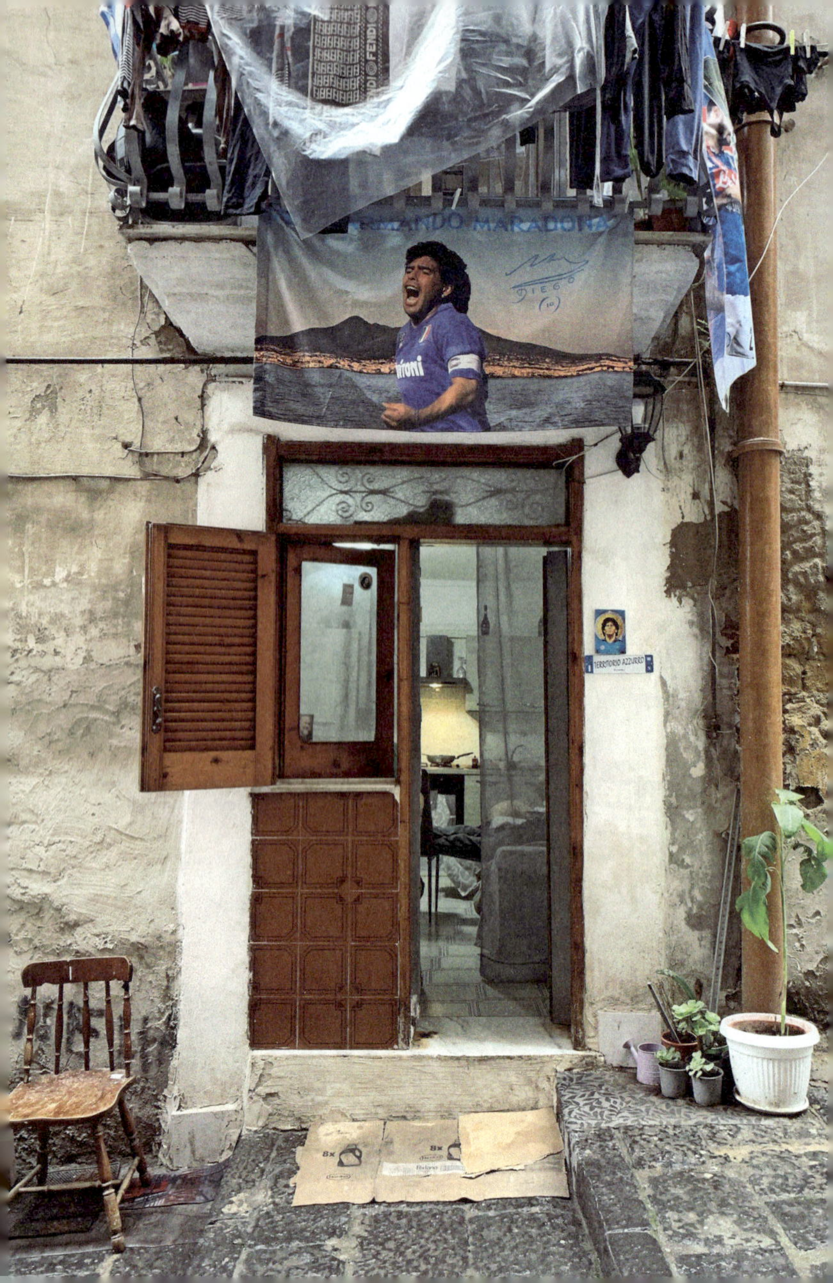
ARMANDO MARADONA
DIEGO
ferroni
TERRITORIO AZZURRO

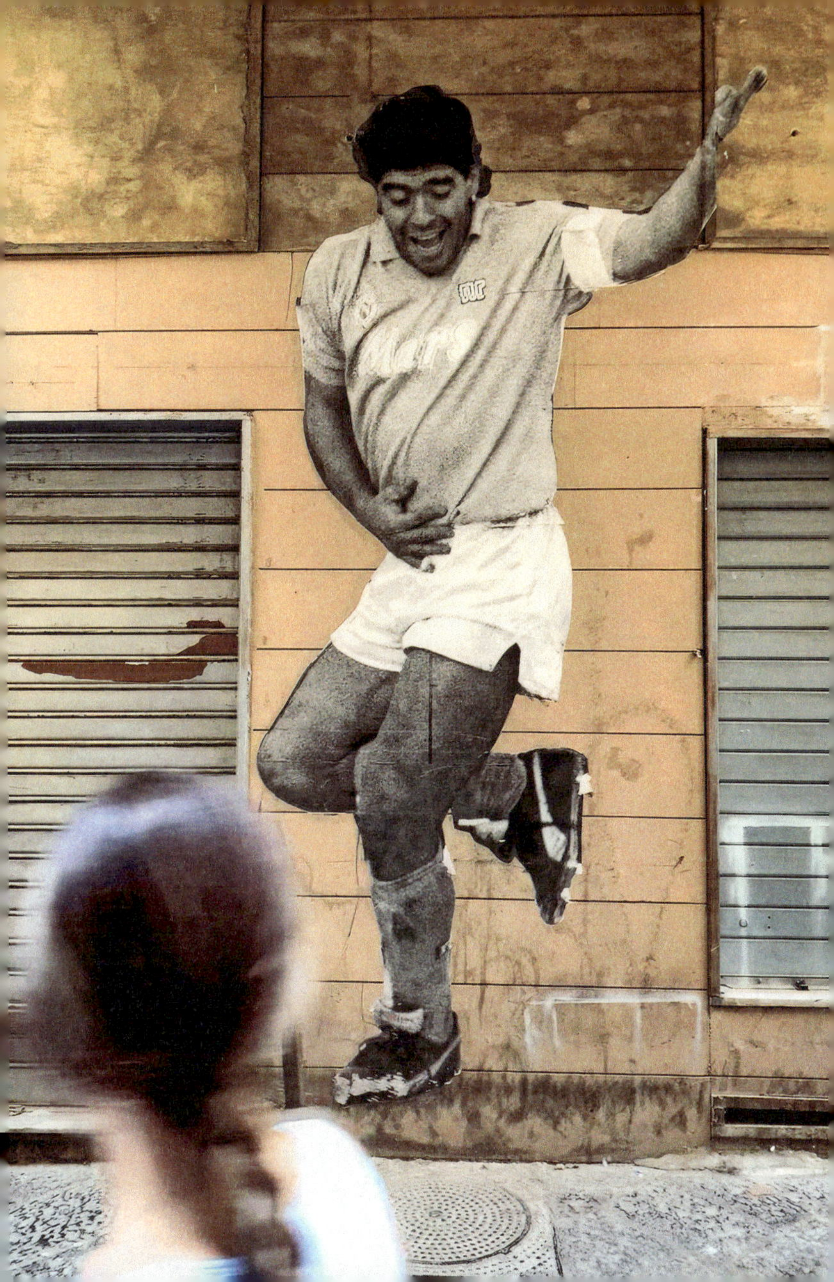

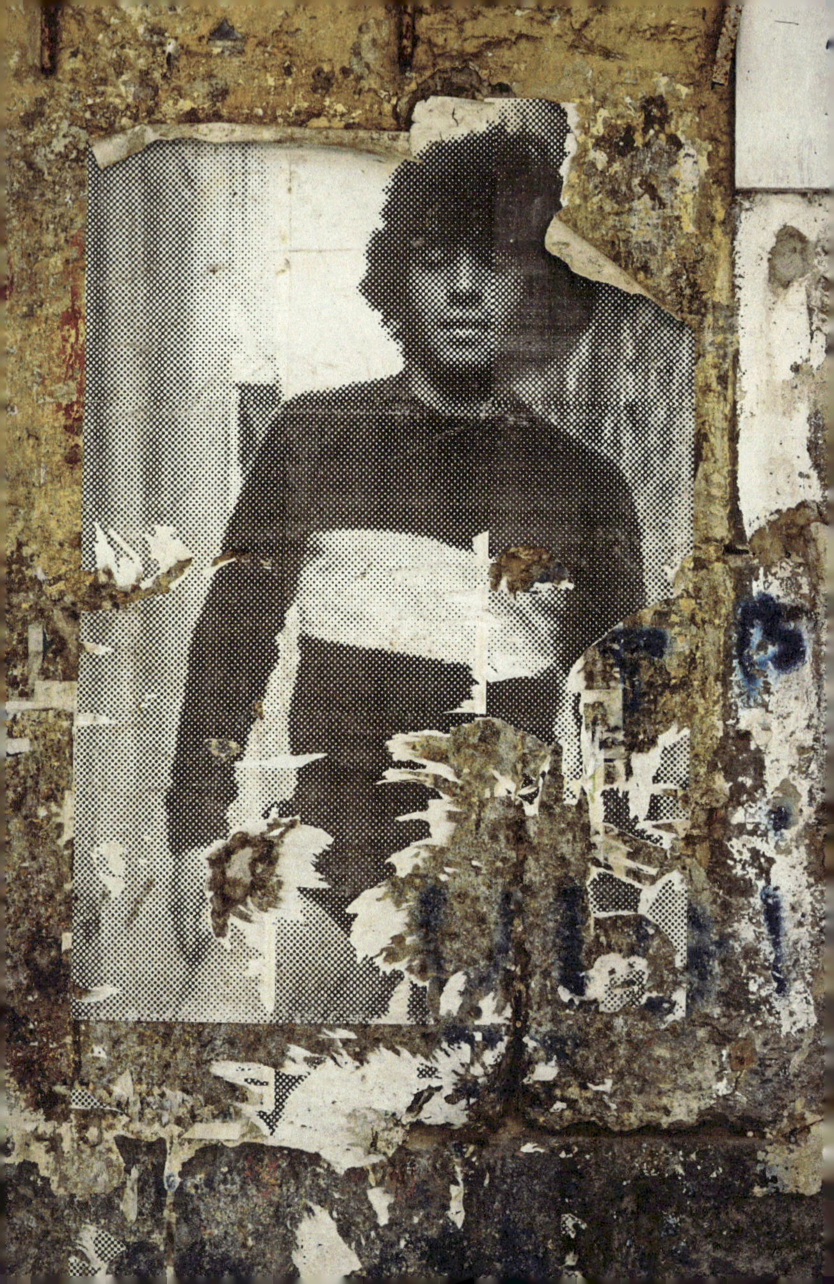

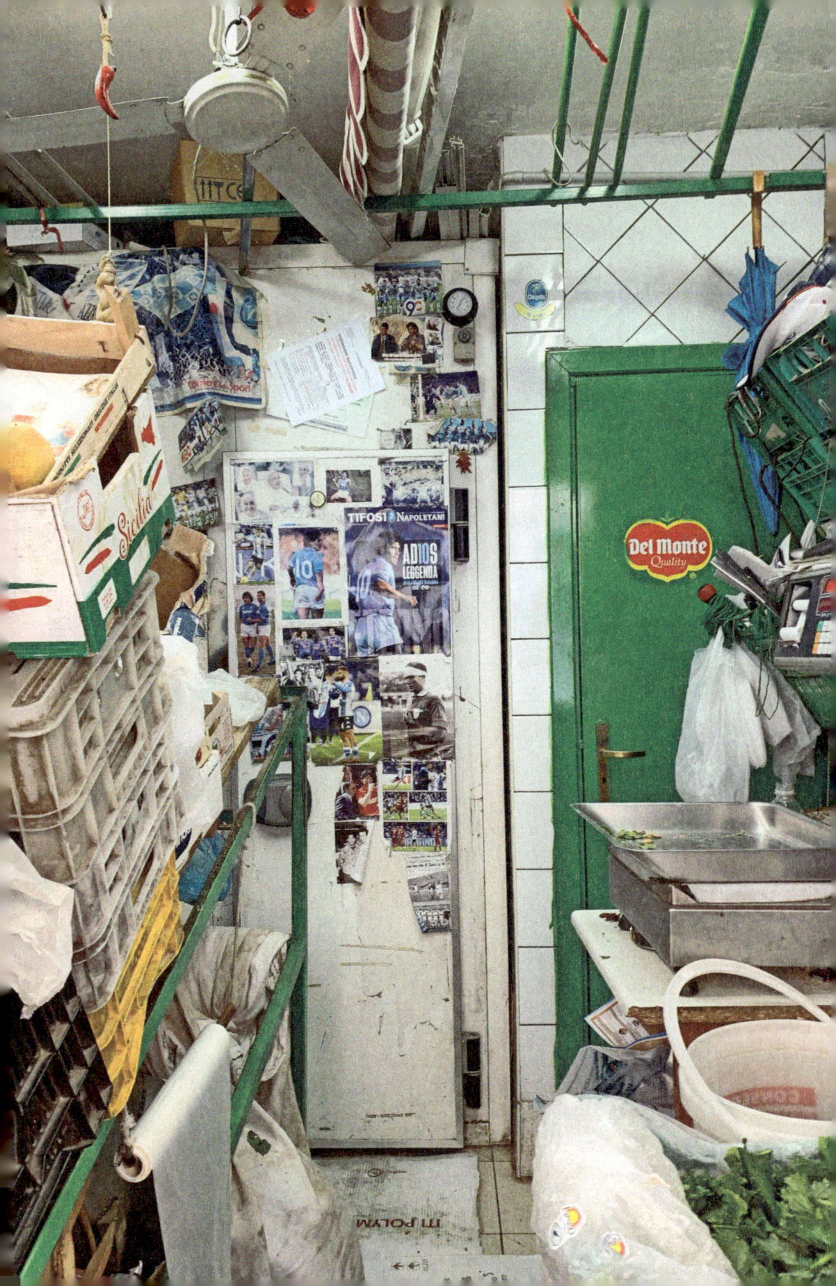

Sicilia
Corriere dello Sport
TIFOSI NAPOLETANI
A D10S
LEGGENDA
Del Monte
Quality

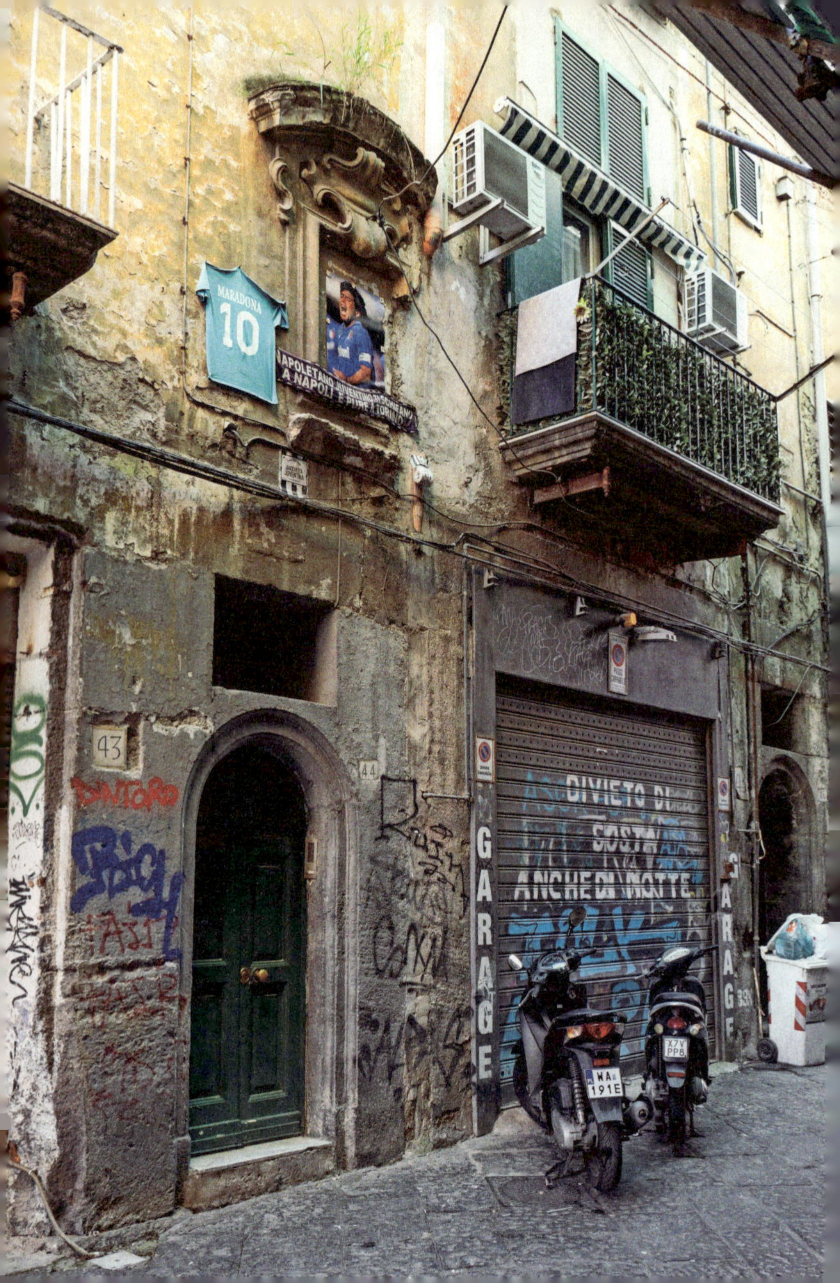

MARADONA
10
NAPOLETANO JUVENTINO SCHIFANO
A NAPOLI E PIUE A TORINO
43
GARAGE
DIVIETO DI
SOSTA
ANCHE DI NOTTE
GARAGE
WA
191E
X7V
PP8

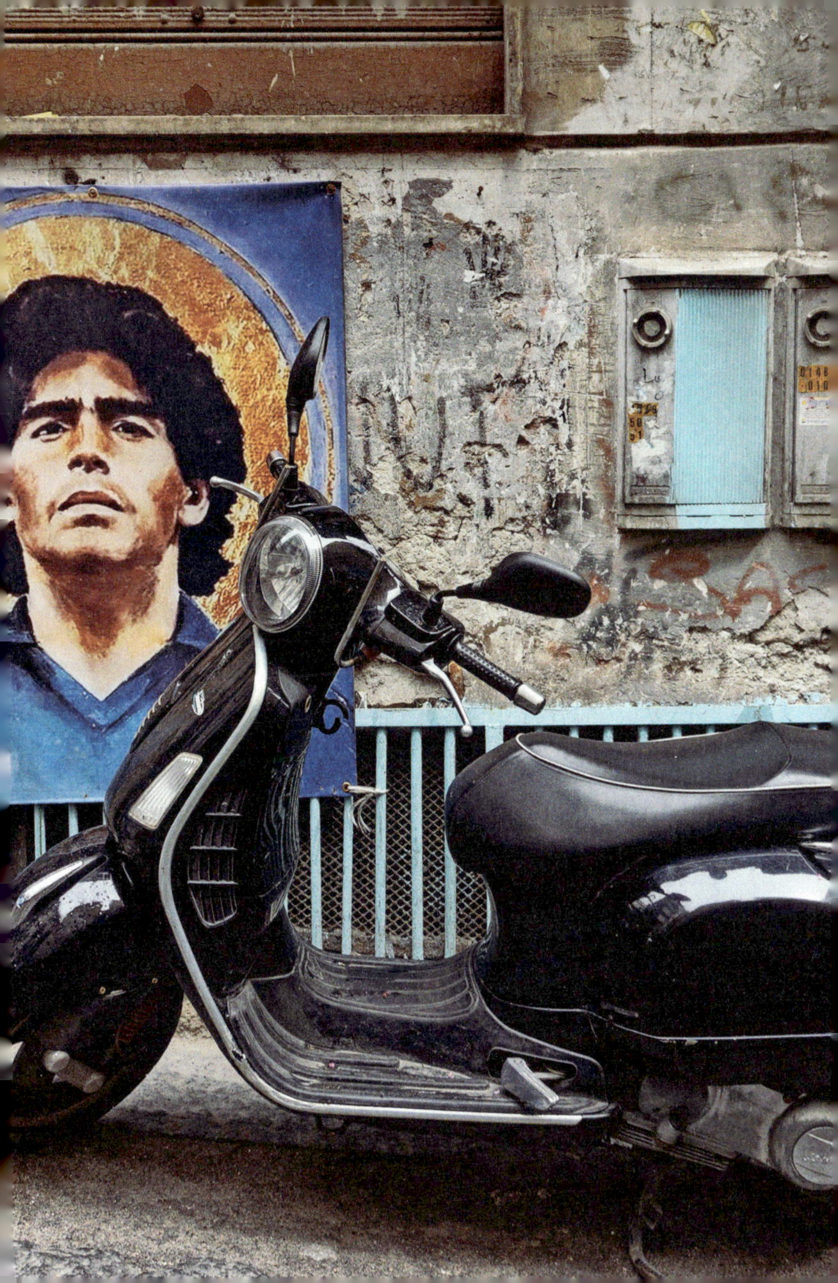

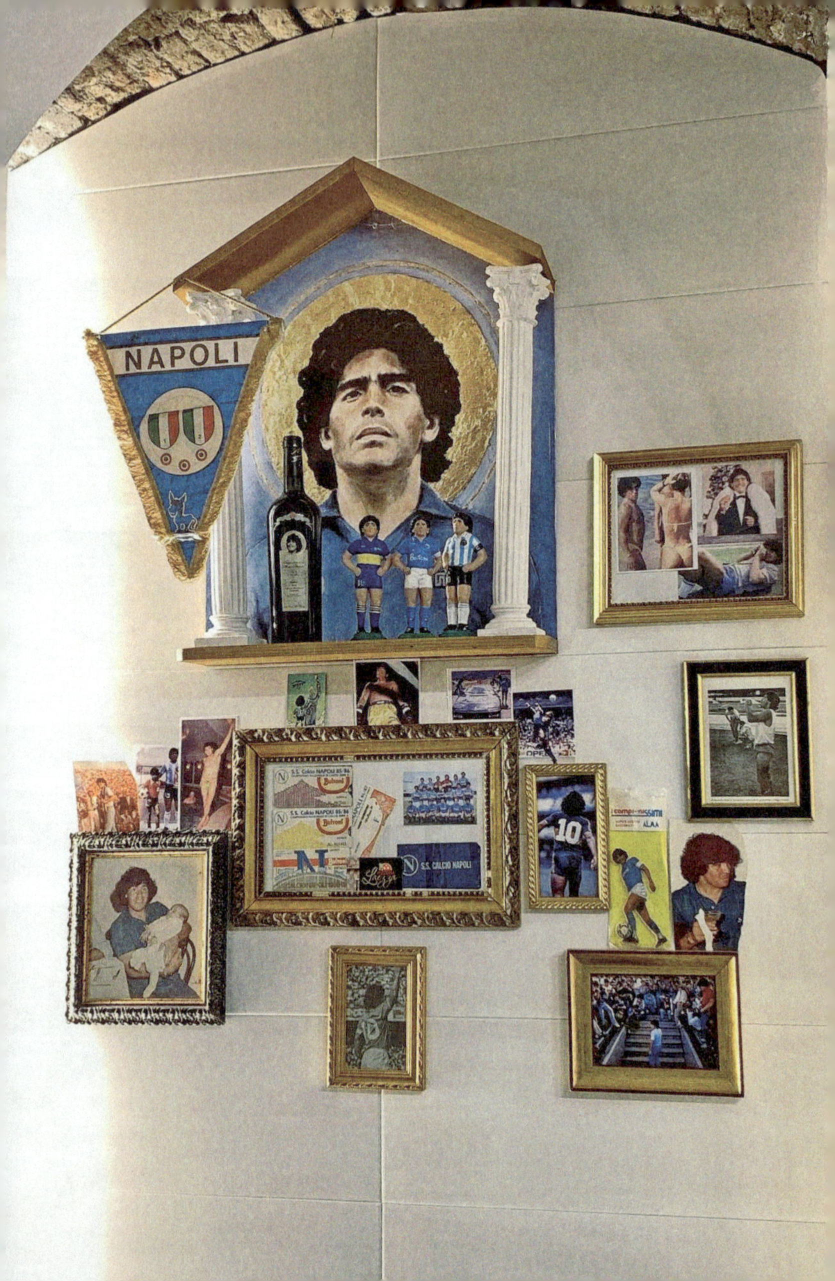

NAPOLI
S.S. CALCIO NAPOLI
10

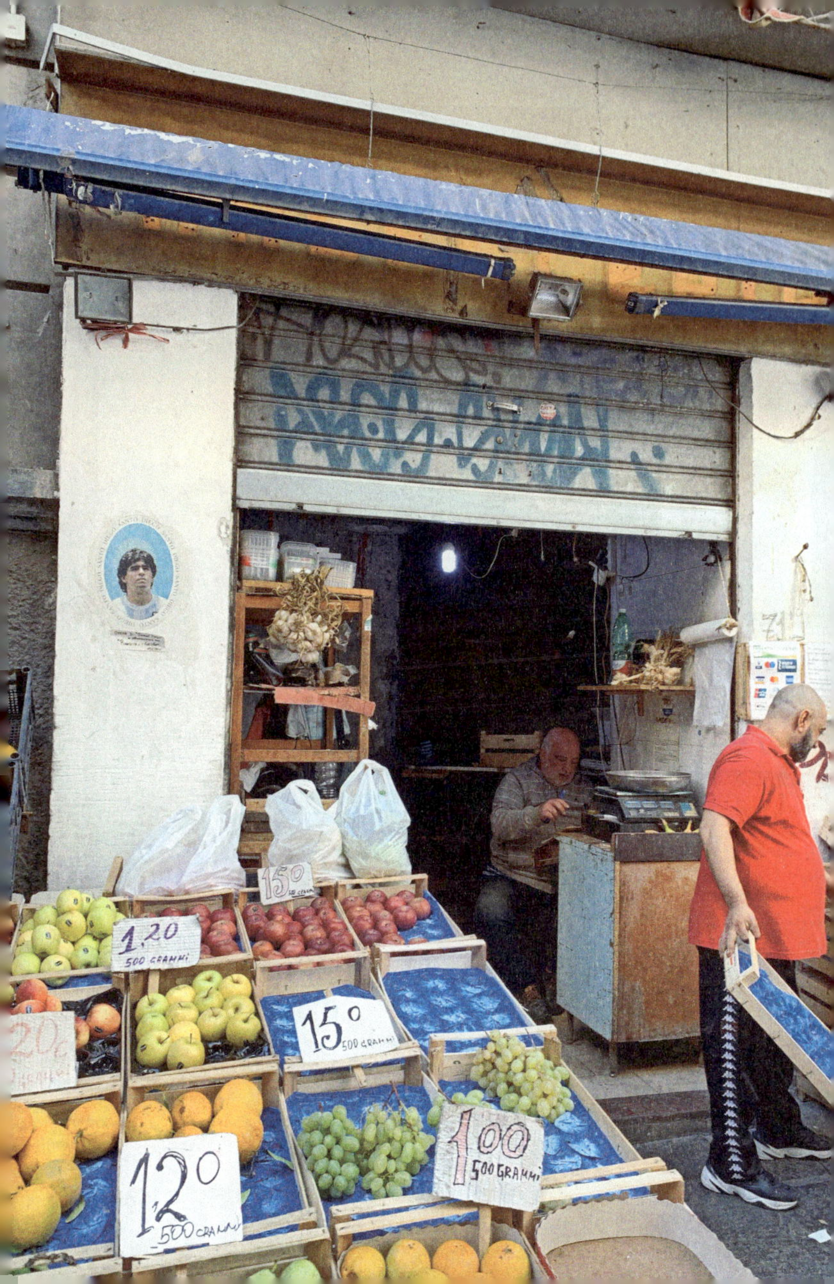
1,20
500 GRAMMI
15°
500 GRAMMI
15°
500 GRAMMI
1°00
500 GRAMMI
1,20
500 GRAMMI

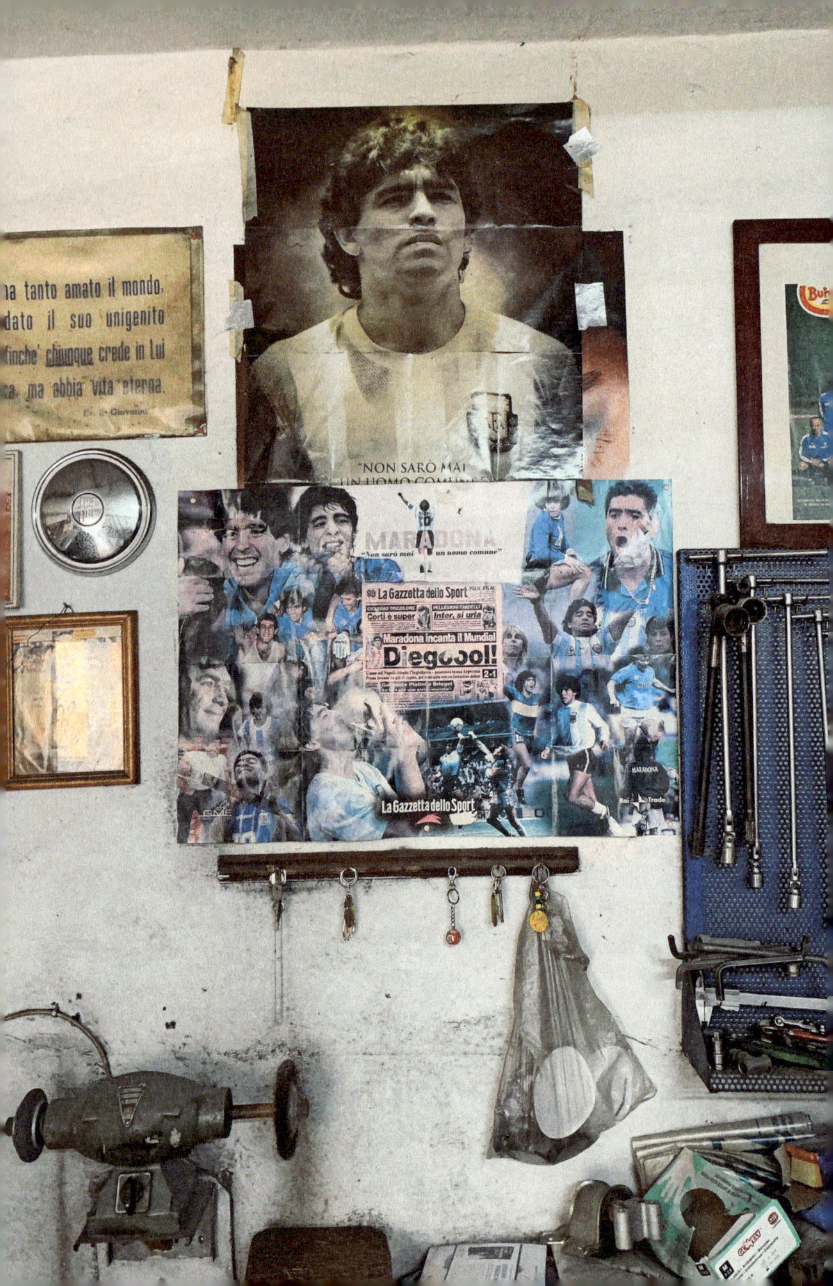
ha tanto amato il mondo,
dato il suo unigenito
finché chiunque crede in Lui
a, ma abbia vita eterna.
Ev. di Giovanni

"NON SARÒ MAI
UN UOMO COMUNE"

MARADONA
"Non sarò mai   un uomo comune"

La Gazzetta dello Sport
CICLISMO TRICOLORE   PELLEGRINI-TARDELLI
Corti è super   Inter, si urla
Maradona incanta il Mundial
Diegooo!!
2-1
La Gazzetta dello Sport

MARADONA

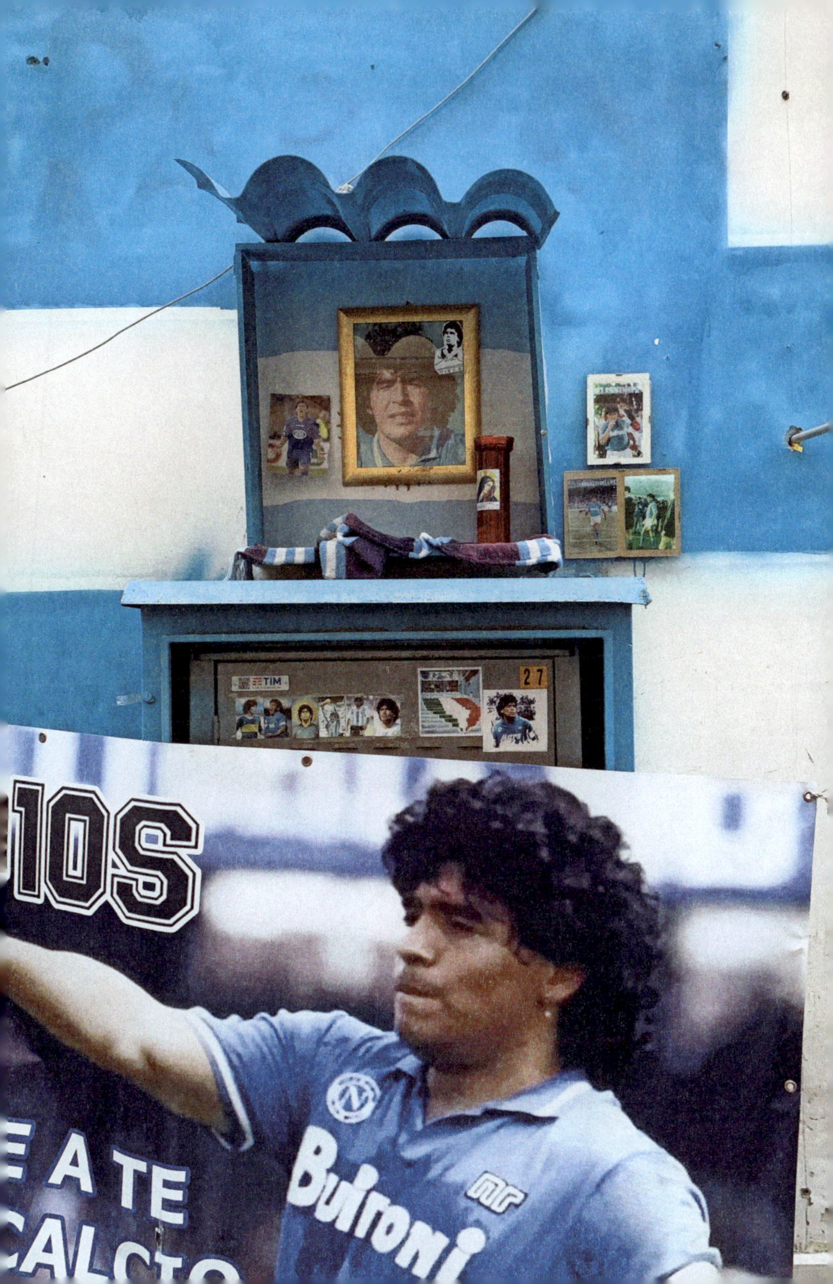
27
TIM
10S
E A TE
CALCIO
Buitoni
nr

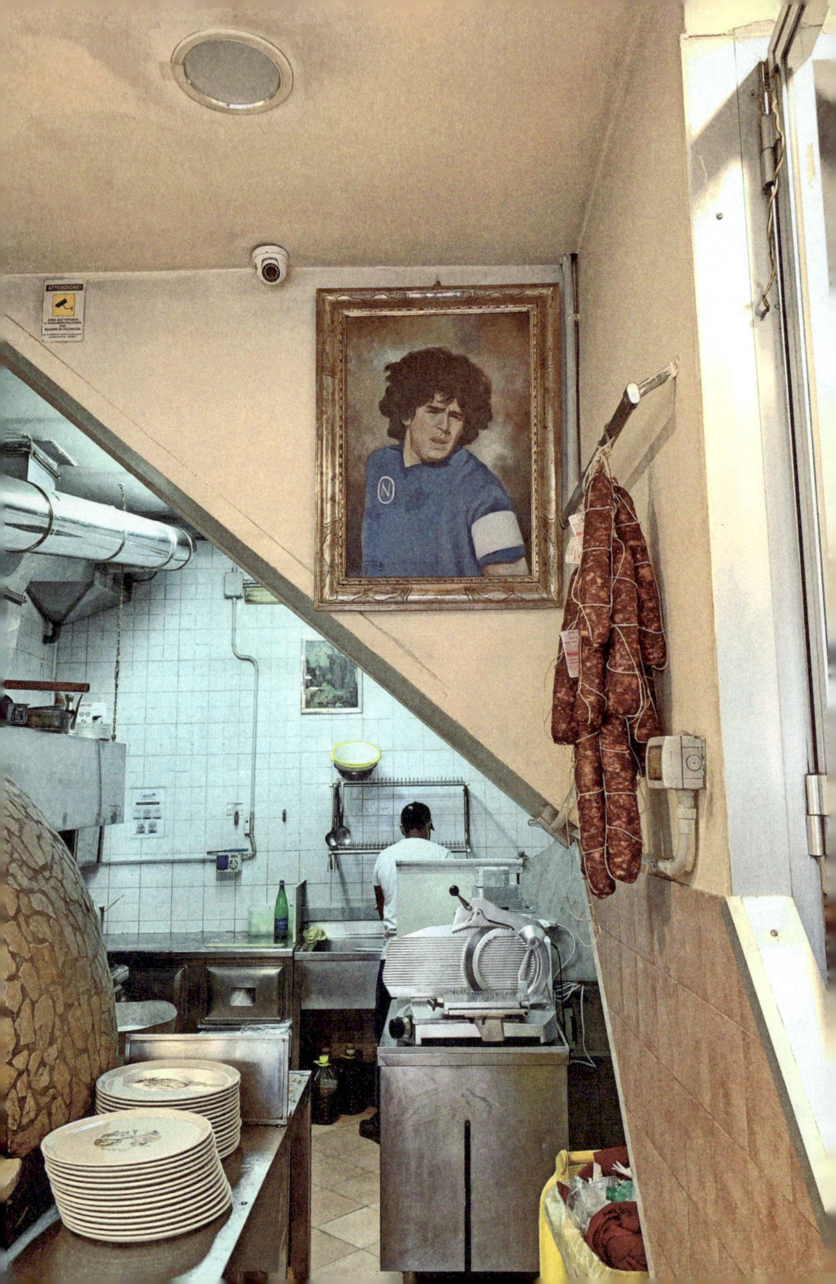

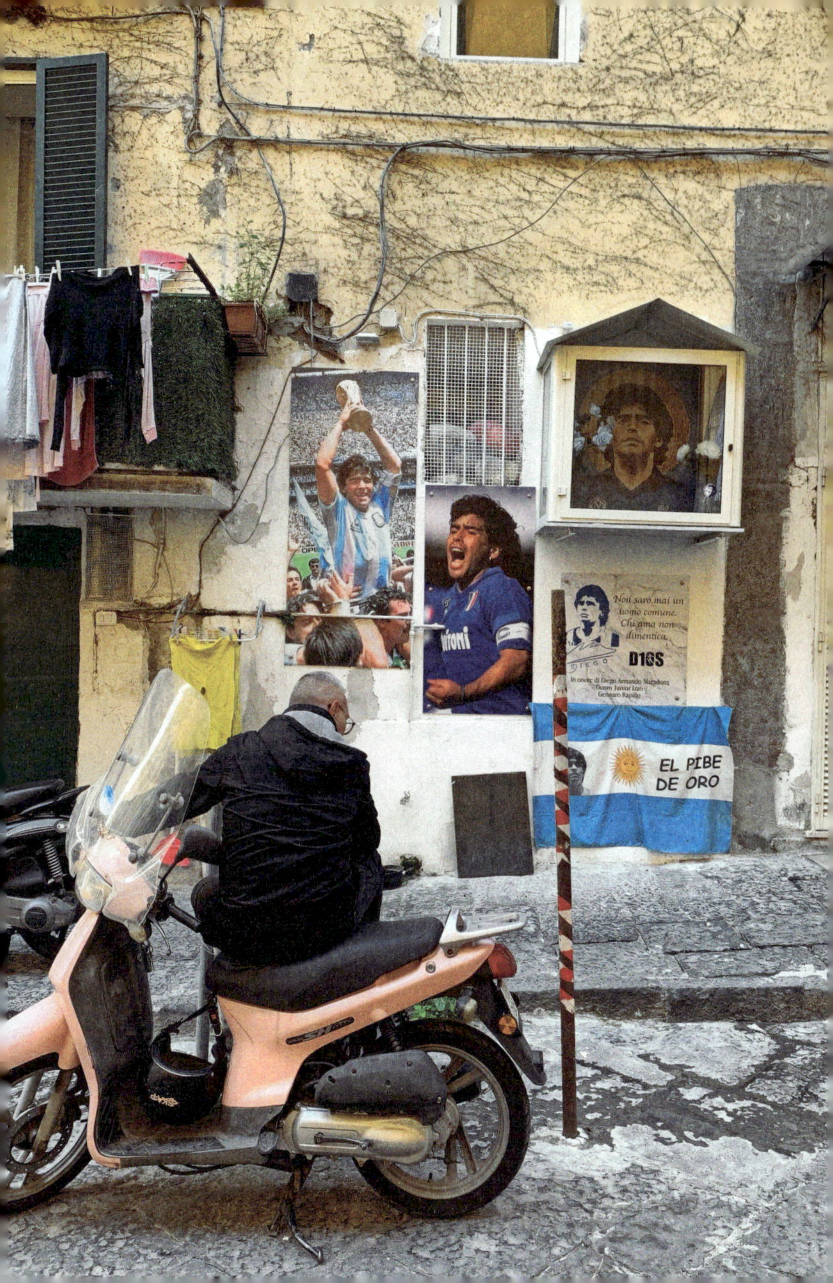
vitomi
Non sarò mai un uomo comune.
Chi ama non dimentica
DIEGO
D10S
In onore di Diego Armando Maradona
EL PIBE
DE ORO

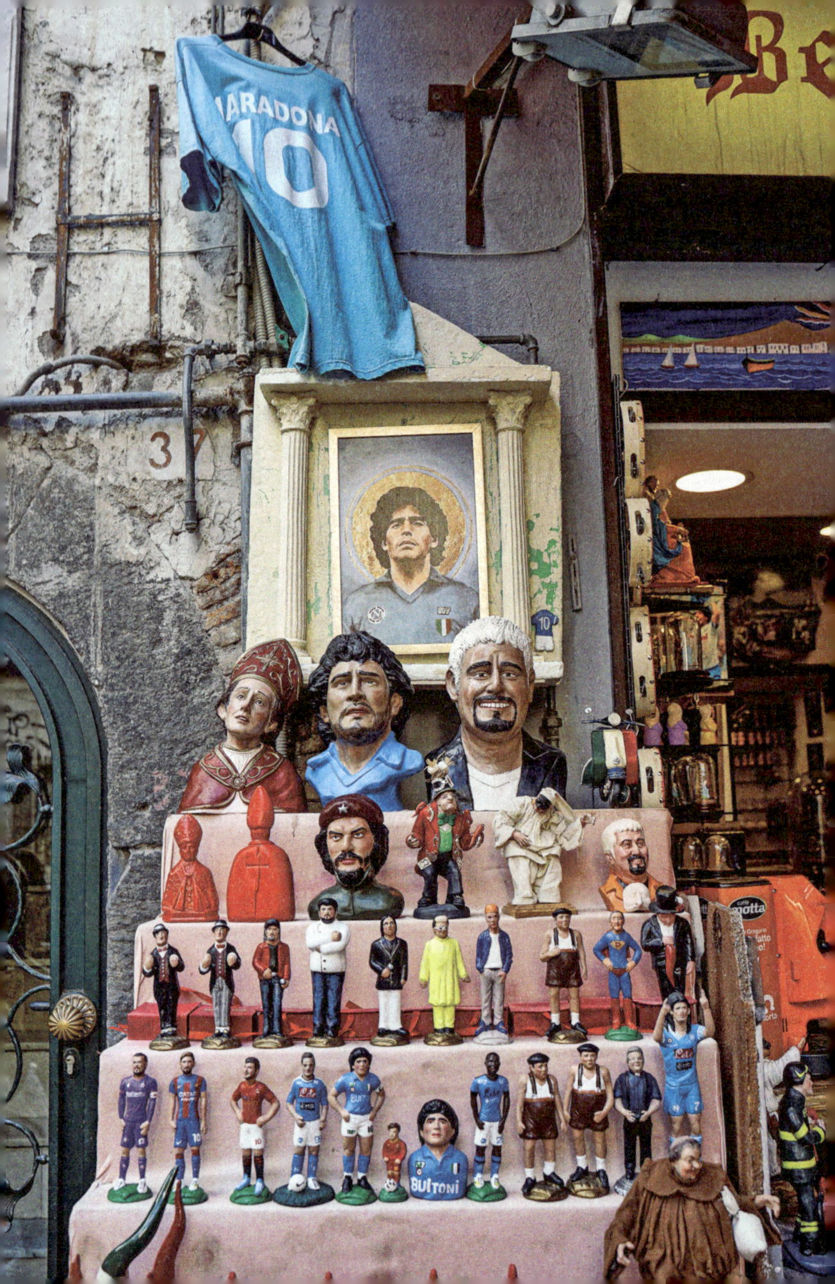
MARADONA
10
37
BUITONI

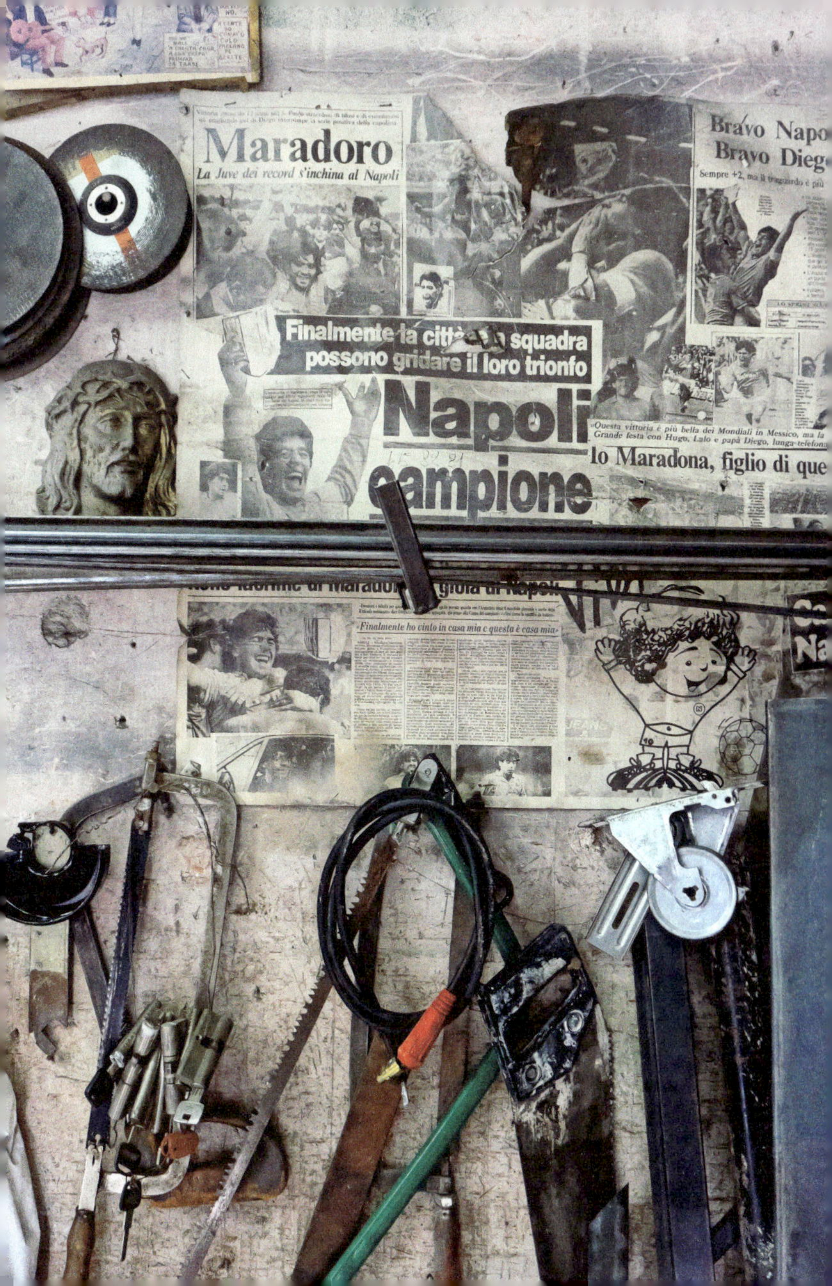

Maradoro
La Juve dei record s'inchina al Napoli
Bravo Napo
Bravo Dieg
Sempre +2, ma il traguardo è più
Finalmente la città e la squadra
possono gridare il loro trionfo
Napoli
campione
«Questa vittoria è più bella dei Mondiali in Messico, ma la
Grande festa con Hugo, Lalo e papà Diego, lunga telefona
lo Maradona, figlio di que
Finalmente ho vinto in casa mia e questa è casa mia

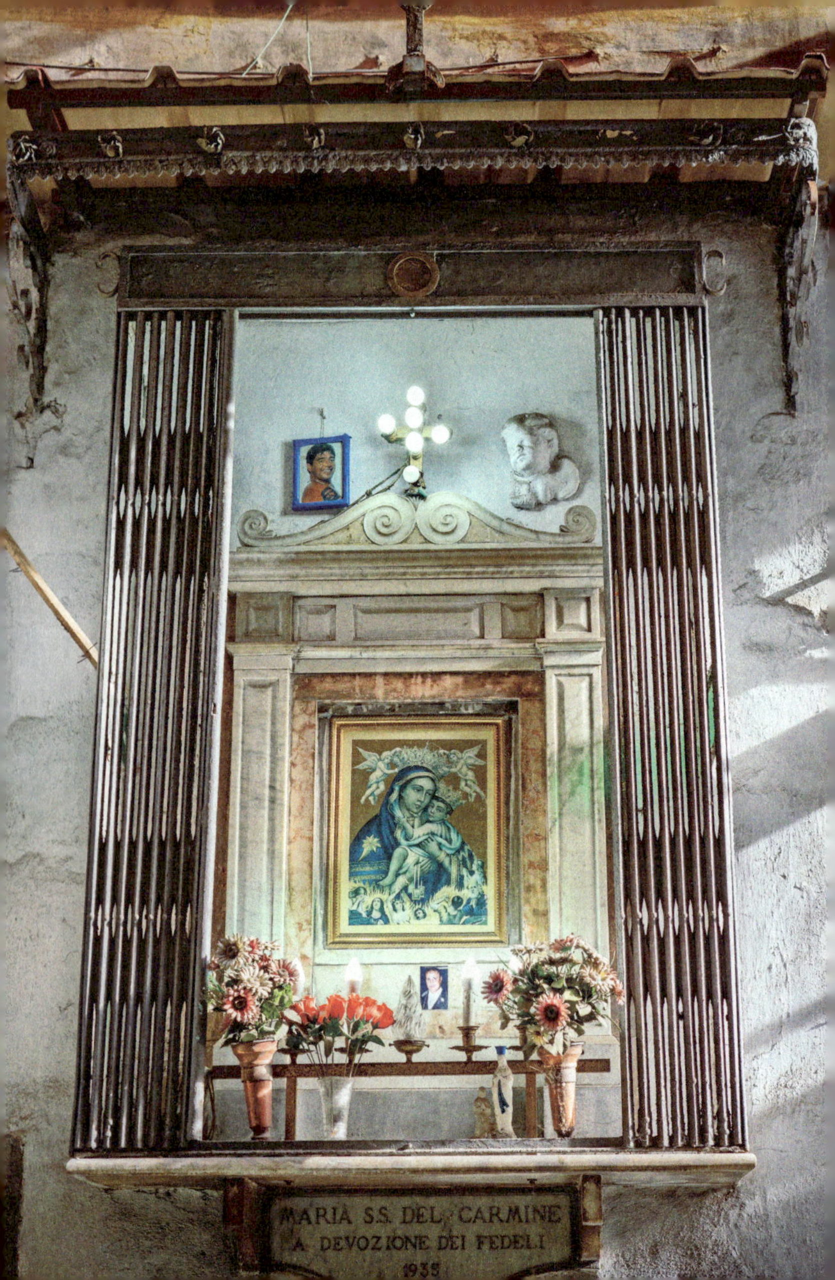

MARIA S.S. DEL CARMINE
A DEVOZIONE DEI FEDELI
1935

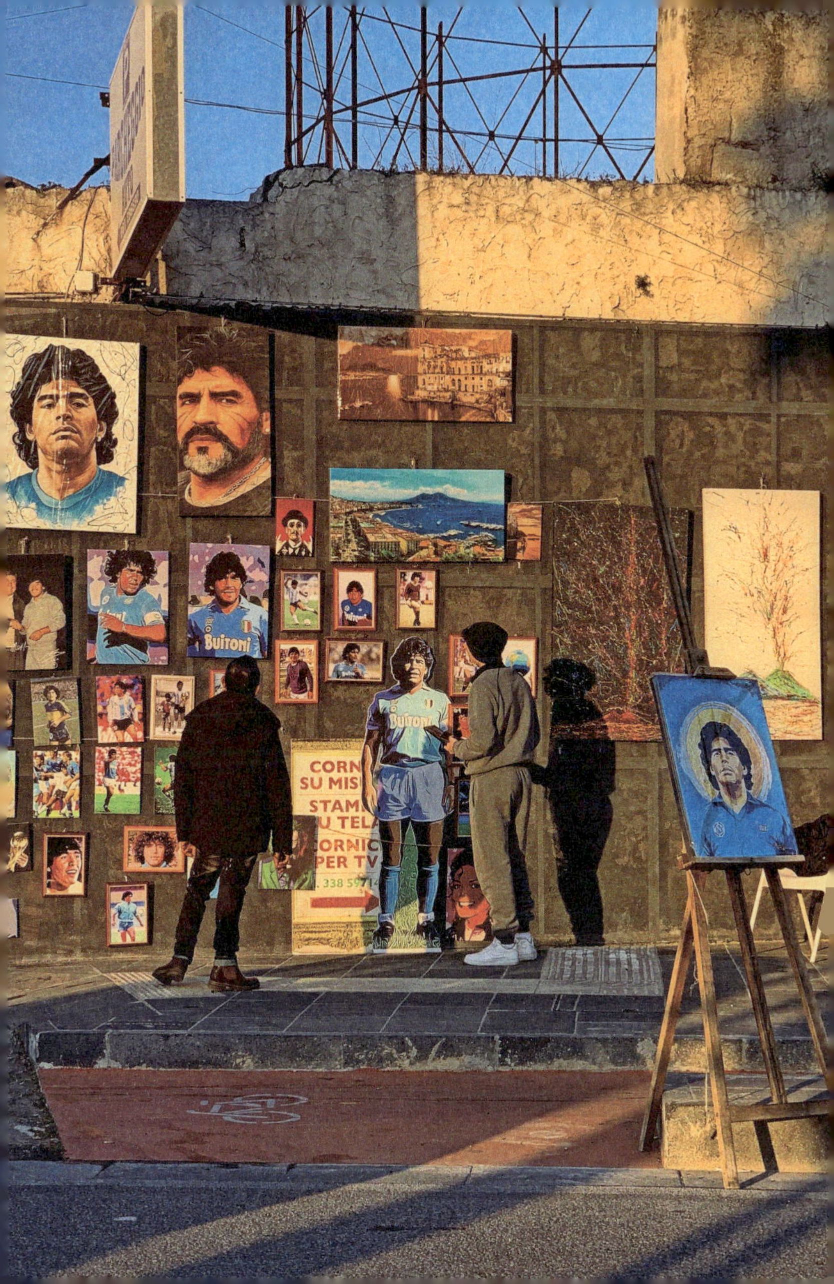

Buitoni
Buitoni
CORN
SU MIS
STAM
U TELA
CORNIC
PER TV
. 338 5971

I Am
One of You

David Diehl
The photographs that precede this chapter were taken by a photographer from Naples. What do we see in them?

Asif Kapadia
I think they paint a great picture of how much the people of Naples love Diego Maradona. I love these images: I've collected so many of these sorts of pictures, old-fashioned cut-outs which were just stuck on a wall somewhere, like in the backroom of a restaurant. You used to see similar cut-out pictures in England when I was younger, in a petrol station or a garage, somebody would've just cut out pictures from the newspaper—you don't see that much anymore. But Naples is so different. It's almost from another time—the intensity of the people, the volcano, the food, the sea. And football. And Diego is the one who they love the most. Even though he's Argentine, it's like he's Neapolitan. I think that's what I see in these photos—a kind of honouring, a kind of religion that makes football what it is.

David Diehl
What kind of city is Naples?

Asif Kapadia
When I was making the film (*Diego Maradona*, 2019), I spent a lot of time there. To understand Diego's effect on the city, we have to go back to the 80s: just before he arrived, there'd been an earthquake, and the city had had to be rebuilt. It was very poor, and

there was a Camorra war going on in the streets; many people were being killed. It was one of the most dangerous places in Europe, one of the poorest places in Europe. It had nothing going for it. All of the wealth was in the north of Italy. And in the middle of all that, they get the best player in the world. Context is everything, isn't it? It's like, 'How the hell does Diego Maradona end up at Napoli?' He joins a team that nearly got relegated, and within three seasons, he wins the Scudetto. So that relationship comes from their status at that time and the context of the media being controlled up in the north, Rome being the 'great city', Milan and all these other places having all the money and the industry and the jobs, their football teams having the best players, and they're looking down on Naples, making fun of Naples. And then: Naples fights back.

Naples now is an amazing, incredible city. But it was a really difficult time in the 80s, and I think that's hard to comprehend—the starting-point that Diego came into, the madness of the city. And then for him to somehow survive that. There's still a kind of intensity in Naples: people get really close to you, in your face. And that's just me or you walking down the street. Imagine what it must have been like for him. I think what we're talking about is Italian passion generally—but Neapolitan passion is on another level.

David Diehl
So Maradona was some kind of a saviour?

Asif Kapadia

He was a saviour. He was a hero. He was a god. He made them proud. He made them happy. And he was proud of that—he needed the fans. They needed him. That's really important—he didn't look down on them. He didn't look at them like, 'I'm better than you.' He was like, 'I'm one of you.' That's what's really important in this story. Diego had come from Barcelona, where they looked down on him, made fun of him, and he hadn't been happy. He'd grown up in Villa Fiorito, a very poor city in Argentina. I've been there, it's pretty scary: no taxi driver would take us there. So: he came from somewhere with real poverty, no electricity, no running water, living in a shack with all of his family. Then he goes from there to Barcelona to be treated really badly. Then he comes to Naples and actually realises: 'I have much more in common with you, and I'm going to fight for you.' And he did. That's why they love him. He fought for them.

David Diehl

I'm especially interested in these religious parallels.

Asif Kapadia

Religion and superstition—all of that is very much a big part of Italy; it's a very superstitious, a very religious landscape. Of course, in Naples San Gennaro and all of the other saints are a very big part of everyday life. Diego is absolutely looked upon as if he was a saint, and that's why the iconography is obviously so important. It isn't a joke. It isn't ironic. They believe in it.

David Diehl

The photographer who took the preceding images is called Alessandro Tione. He was born in 1998: he never saw Maradona play himself. He grew up in a city which from his point of view is always harking back to a glorified past. Why does Diego not depart Naples? What does Maradona mean to the young people that they still sing songs about him?

Asif Kapadia

It's a different level of devotion. It's hard to comprehend for most people because many teams, including Napoli, have had lots of great players over the years. However, I don't think there has ever been anyone quite like Diego. Nobody, *nobody* now would ever go to a team like Napoli, and help them come out of nowhere to reach the heights. That team had nearly got relegated, and he helped them win the toughest title in the world. So, there's always been this idea of him being this character who took on the rest of the country, took on Juventus, took on Milan, took on Inter. He helped them win the Scudetto—and then they never won it again until 2023, and they've had a really difficult time in the intervening decades. And so he's been elevated to this position, to this mythical godlike character who took this team and this city that has always been fighting against the north, always fighting for respect, to the top. He gave them respect. What you see in Alessandro's photos is exactly this kind of love. People in Naples have two images above their beds: Jesus and Diego.

A lot of this happened when it wasn't on TV around the world, and that's why the myth and the stories are important. It's people's parents and grandparents telling stories to their kids. Not everyone was there in the stadium to see Diego play. But the stories almost become more beautiful because there wasn't television and the Internet and social media at the time. So it's like history that has been handed down. People still name their sons Diego. He was the guy who helped them win in Europe. He was the guy who put them on the map.

David Diehl

I think these desires, these dreams of the people connected to their football clubs are something special. Is that something only football can create? Or is there any other form of pop culture that has a similar thing going on?

Asif Kapadia

Football's the thing. Wherever you go in the world, it's the sport that brings people together. It's basically the sport of the ordinary people, the poor people around the world. You don't need much to play football. You don't need a lot of equipment, and you can always get enough people together to kick something about, even if you don't have a ball. So all of Latin America and Central America and now North America, with Messi going there, has been taken over. There and in all of Africa, all of Asia, all of Europe—everyone plays football. And within that context, you have a sport that's covered on television: the World Cup, the

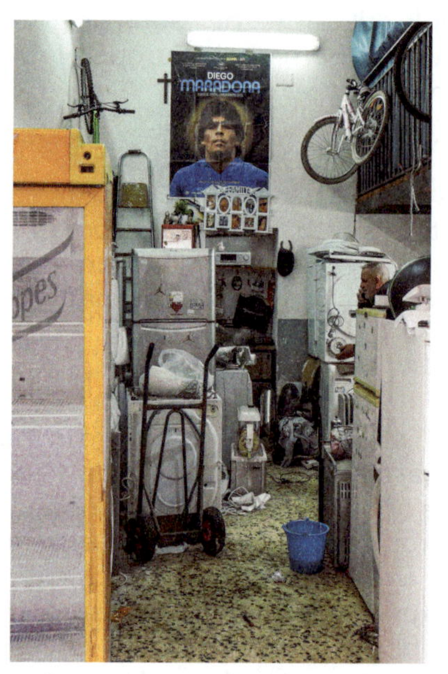

DIEGO
MARADONA

different leagues. I don't think there's anything that's as big as football. And then, if you're great at football, you'll become elevated around the world.

David Diehl

Who's your team?

Asif Kapadia

I'm a Liverpool fan.

David Diehl

But you're from London, aren't you?

Asif Kapadia

It's terrible, isn't it? But I've been Liverpool fan since the 70s. My family were all Arsenal. I grew up near the stadium, but I've always been a Liverpool fan.

I have to say, part of my relationship with Naples is that it's very similar to Liverpool. Both Liverpool and Naples were important port cities with great histories, which national governments in both countries repeatedly ignored over the decades, letting the cites become poorer so the local people suffered incredible poverty, which leads to crime. This created in both cites a massive distrust of those in power. Historically a lot of people used to make fun of them for being poor. And they've got this feeling that they're always the underdog. Liverpool hadn't won the title for a very long time, since 1990—until Klopp came along. And then that feeling was the same. Both Liverpool and Napoli won the championship so long ago and then had thirty years of suffering.

David Diehl
You met Diego. What kind of person was he? Did he still exist as a person, or was he just a guy who had taken on a role from the very beginning?

Asif Kapadia
Very interesting question. I met a person who had very different moods depending on the day you met him. He had good days and not-so-good days. And when he was charming, he was very charming and very sweet and very nice. On other days, when he was in a bad mood, I didn't want to be around him.

And then when I was making the film, I was seeing the footage of this young guy—happy, smiling, a joyful person and player. So in the film I ended up coming up with this concept of two characters. There's Diego, and there's Maradona. That became the way to understand the psychology of somebody who has this innocent and joyful side, but also has this very tough side, who knows his work—the ego-driven version. That was how I understood him, how I portrayed him in the film. I would say that I met 'Maradona', but I never met 'Diego', the kid, because the person I was meeting was older and had been through so many things. I don't know if he remembered the kid. To be honest, I don't know if he could remember, because of all the stuff that he'd been through, and also what he'd done to himself: the various addictions, the problems that he'd had. It was sometimes quite difficult to dig back into his own memories. So it's hard to get past that, but I did try to do so with the film—to try to get a different answer to the one you would've seen everywhere else. But it was amazing to be there. Who knew that a few years later he wouldn't be around anymore.

David Diehl

Let's talk about pictures. I'm interested in your opinion, because both of us use pre-existing images in our work. Are they like meta-works? Pictures on pictures? My work is very specifically about merging a pictorial tradition with new content. This creates something new, something that's more than just the sum of its parts. Is there a relation here to your work?

Asif Kapadia

I definitely think so. In the end, what we're both doing is almost like a version of Pop Art. And how I create a portrait, I would say, is like a mosaic. The material I work with already exists. You do as much research as possible, to try to understand the psychology, and then you go around the world finding little bits of whatever you can find that have a little bit of the essence of a character, and then you put them all together. So that when you step away, you see the full picture of a person. And it's all made out of fragments. With *Diego Maradona* some of the fragments we found in Argentina, in Buenos Aires, some we found in Florida, some we found in different parts of the US. We found some in Spain, in Barcelona, and then we found some in Naples. We found some outside Naples, and some in Milan. In our case it's audio and visual fragments, and then my job is to work with my team to put it all together to make it feel like one portrait of one human being. I guess in a way what we're both doing is almost like a version of a pop-up. I would say it's taking some pre-existing thing and then putting yourself into it, giving it a context in a different framing, a different hit of colour and meaning that makes it something new.

David Diehl

But where does the truth lie? Is there a complete picture? Or in the end is it a universal story being told, which uses Diego—or Amy Winehouse—as a model? Isn't it inevitably a transformation of the content?

Asif Kapadia

Absolutely it is. In the end, it's an opinion. Someone else could do a version of *Diego Maradona* or *Amy* (2015) and they would make a very different film. Someone else could make a film about Maradona with the same material and say it was the most amazing, fun time a man has ever had. But I saw a sort of sadness. I thought it wasn't fun, actually. He was quite a troubled person who'd been through some very difficult things. I suppose that was the theme running through the three films that I did: all of them—Ayrton Senna, Amy, Diego—were very young when they became famous. And that's challenging. Each of them was fighting a system, or fighting corruption, trying to take it on, but each of them, in their own way, loses. But that's my point of view. And am I projecting onto them, or am I getting it only from what I think they have experienced?

156

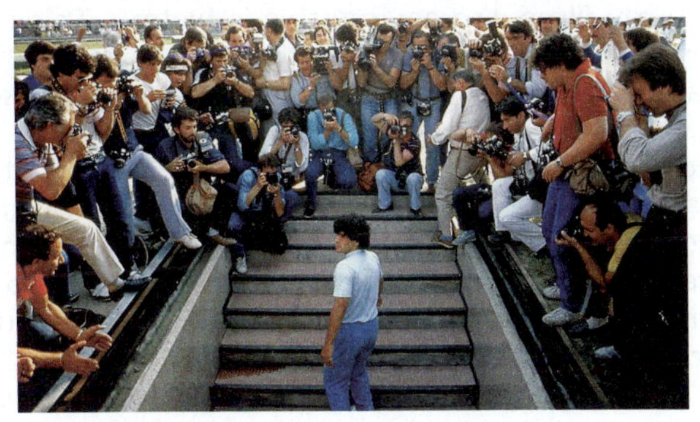

Anyway, when you hand it over, the audience will have their own interpretation. And that's fine.

David Diehl
Absolutely. What touched me the most about your film was that it showed that fragility of Diego. We hadn't seen before. It certainly wasn't about glorifying his character. It's a multi-layered, ambivalent portrait—and ultimately a film about something much bigger and more universal than a single person.

Asif Kapadia
With my films, I'm saying: this is history. This is a period of time. This is a location. But *Senna* (2010) is as much about Brazil as it is about him being a racing driver. It's actually not about racing cars: it's also about another spiritual kind of journey that the characters are on. And *Amy* is about her, but it's also very much a film about London and everything I love about London—everything I hate about it too, in terms of how we treat people here, how pop culture and the tabloids and the media work.

And I love football. But with *Diego Maradona* I also wanted to talk about how it can destroy kids, take them and chew them up. Give them money and power at such a young age, and then say: 'It's your problem that you've become an addict—it's nothing to do with us.' Then move on to the next kid. I wanted to talk about how racism exists in Italy even between Italians. I wanted to talk about things that people had never really talked about before, about the songs that people sing and how awful they are.

All of this is to give a sense of Italy and a sense of football and sport and culture, as well as being a portrait of a little human being. I was dealing with a lot of bigger issues, definitely.

David Diehl
Let's talk about my icon for a moment, which is the main subject of this book.

Asif Kapadia
You know what's really interesting? When people I know go to Naples, they see your image of Diego Maradona somewhere there and then they send me photographs of it. So I get sent your image, because of the film. When I saw the image I always thought it was super-cool, because I always had the idea in my mind that he's an icon. If you look at the poster for our film I think it may even be we had a similar idea, before I'd seen your image of it, with the halo.

David Diehl
Somebody from your research team might have seen it already—I found an email in my inbox from 2017 where I was asked about the availability of the original icon in connection with the film project. But then that fizzled out.
But claiming the originality of this idea doesn't lead anywhere interesting, because most likely there were representations of Diego with a halo before my icon and before your film. The question instead is this: why do some images work better than others? This painting has had a career, by my standards.

Asif Kapadia

There are for sure iconic images. And of course they spread all over the world: specifically in sport there are images—of Muhammad Ali, Pelé and many others—which are definitely iconic.

What's interesting about your painting is that he's not actually kicking the ball. It's just him looking out. I don't know if this was the reference, but for me it's very much like he's lining up before a match. Probably from the Argentina–England game in 1986: he's so determined to beat England, he wants to get revenge against them, post-Falklands War, that he makes a particular face to the camera. Even when it's about sport, you're always dealing with geopolitics, with all of the wider-world stuff, and that image that you've used is him in the line-up saying, basically, 'Fuck you, I'm Maradona—just you try and come for me.' There's some sort of defiance in there that's really strong. And the big hair. And that kit is a really great kit.

David Diehl

That's interesting, and also confirms something you mentioned earlier: the viewer always completes the story himself—with his point of view, his background, his own history. The reference photo for the Maradona icon is not from the England game. I know that picture, and I see absolutely what you're saying and what that context is about. But I believe that it's more than that. In the *Icons* series, there are indeed pictures that are based on a single reference photo—but not the Maradona one. There the eyes, hair, mouth, kit are all put together from different

160

sources. In this sense, the artistic circle of making a portrait is closed again: it's a mosaic, composed of different parts, which all make up a part of the whole. Part of what I would call 'my Maradona'.

Last question… The 80s were definitely a different time: there were far fewer images about than we're confronted with today. Was that why they were stronger? Did the photos of 'Maradona' do something to 'Diego'?

Asif Kapadia
Of course, people were making flags and banners at home and bringing them to the stadium, or hanging them outside their houses in the narrow streets of Naples, painting murals on the sides of buildings, and everywhere you went you'd see the Napoli flag and you'd see Diego's image. And then these cut-outs from the newspapers that we talked about before were a big part of it: the local newspapers were where you got your information from, and they'd have photos of him in there every day, and the Neapolitans would cut them out. And people would paint murals on the side of buildings. At the time it was simple, a little cut-out put behind a piece of glass—which becomes a kind of icon that they stuck up on the wall. That's the charm of it, in a way. When you go to those Neapolitan bars that have a little corner dedicated to Diego, the images are not flashy images, they're quite simple. That's the beauty of it, isn't it? A little picture that is loved.

I think that he would've seen all that and it would've all given him strength. But I'd also say that in terms of his particular experience, it's also part of the reason why he went a bit crazy and had to leave Naples. Because in a way it's amazing ... but you're not a god. You're an ordinary person, and it can drive you crazy. It's the danger of having everything and being treated like a god when you're not. When you're mortal.

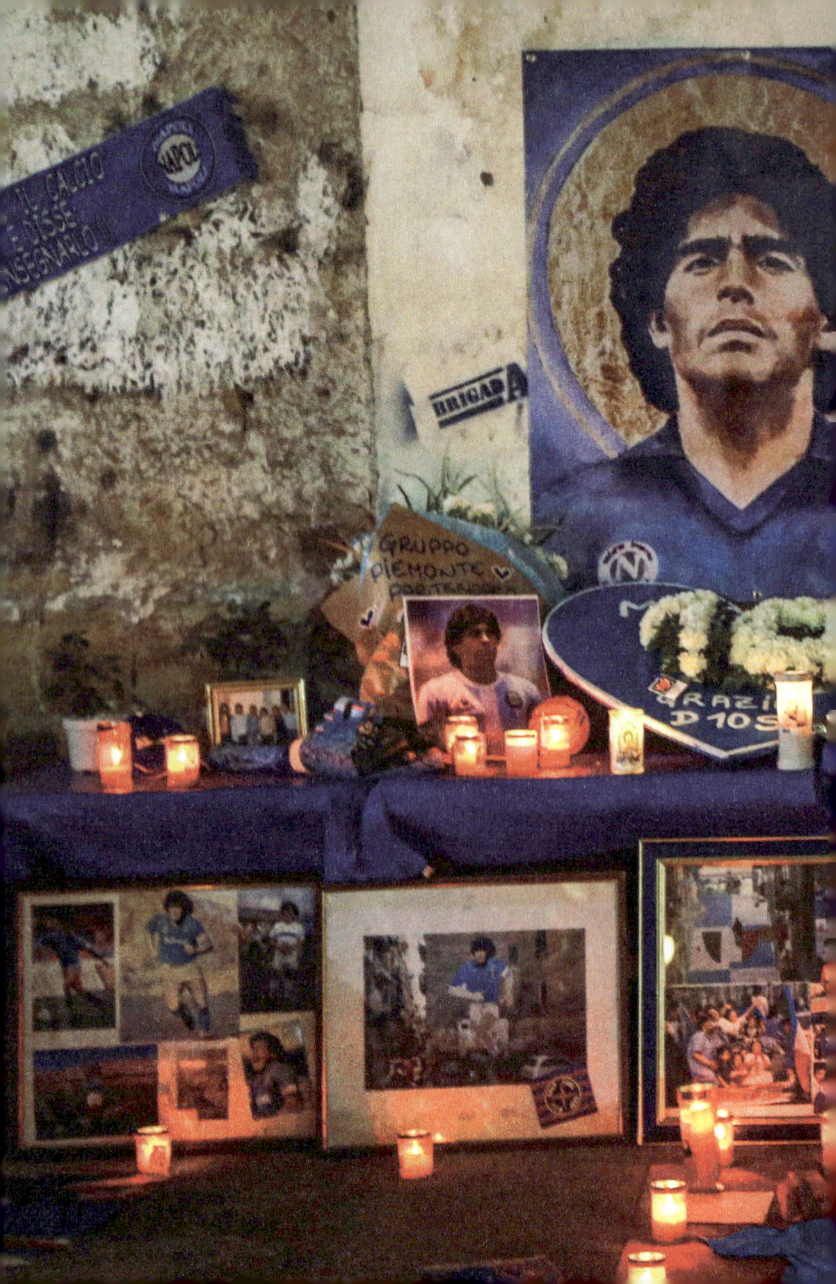

IL CALCIO
E DISSE
INSEGNARLO !!
NAPOL
BRIGAD
GRUPPO
PIEMONTE
GRAZIE
D 10 S

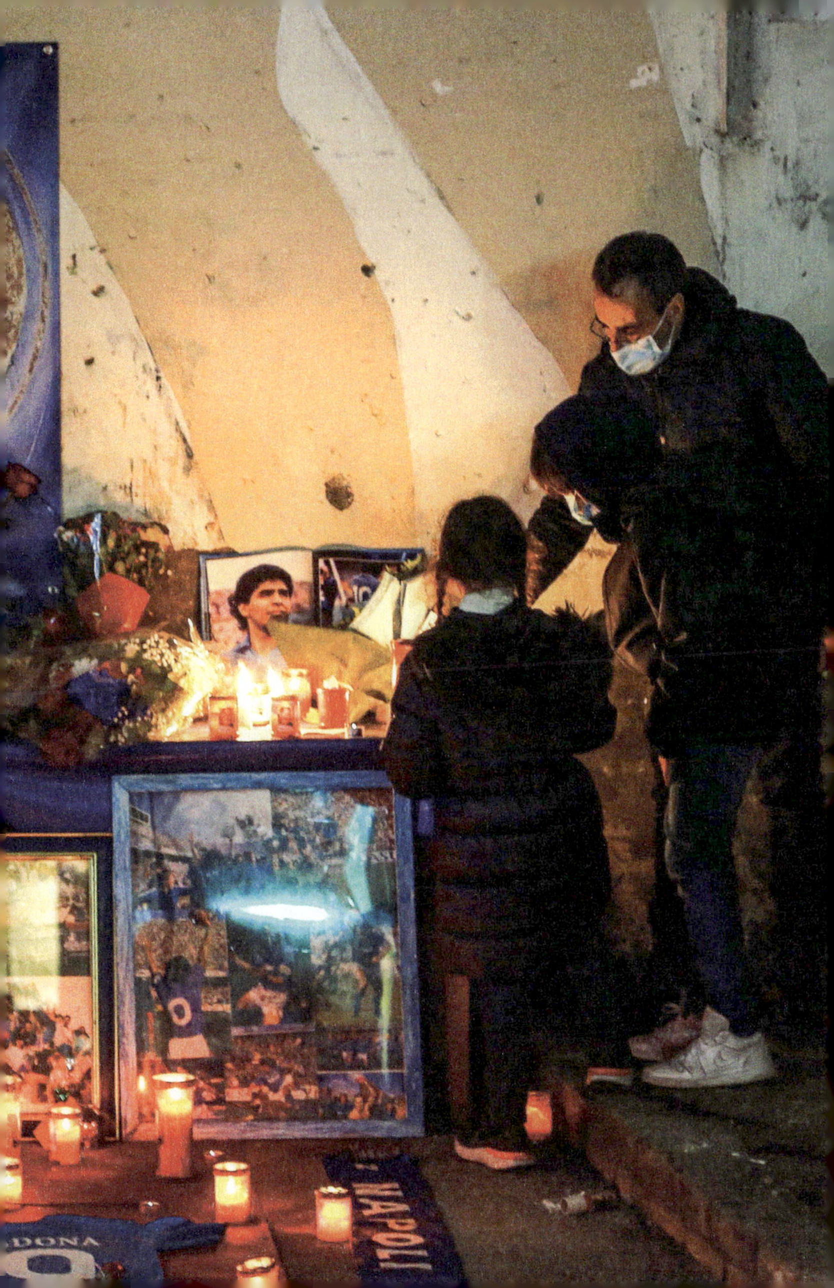

Text and Photographs by David Diehl

Venerdí Santo e Pasqua

Over Easter I returned to Naples for the first time in a long time, to see what has become of my Diego.

Naples was all abuzz that Easter, its city centre streets more packed than ever as the first warm days of spring coincided with religious festivals and fused with excitement about Napoli's first shot at the championship title since 1991. The *napoletani* really couldn't wait any longer. Although there were still more than ten matches to go that season, Napoli's lead over Lazio was already too big to lose this chance at a third Scudetto. *Napoli campione, Napoli tre!* The whole city, every street corner and every alley, was festooned with flags, garlands, shirts. I hadn't expected this, nor had I ever experienced so much exuberance. *Calcio* is more than just football and a Scudetto in Napoli is more than a championship title in any other sport. And there's more to it in another sense: it's the south rebelling against the overpowering north, against its disdain and disregard. That was true in the late 80s and it's still true today. Which is why people associate Diego with more than just romantic football memories or glorified childhood experiences. Alighting in Naples as if out of the blue, Maradona went on to earn the city two championship titles—as well as some measure of respect and recognition—for which the Neapolitans are forever grateful. *Onore a colui che a fatto la nostra storia: Diego Armando Maradona.*

And now this rebirth! After all the financial and licensing problems and relegation to Serie C, SSC Napoli

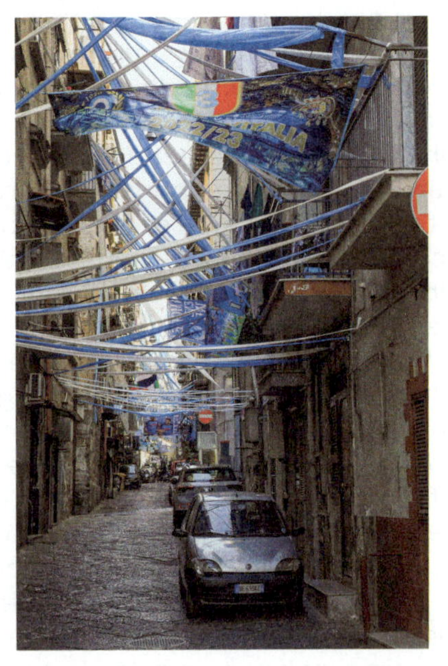

have been back amongst the Serie A frontrunners for years now—and now this: a third Scudetto within reach, transforming Eastertide Naples at the close of the 2022–2023 season into a torrent of unbridled exhilaration in sky blue and white.

And there, smack in the thick of it, my Diego. On every corner, at every stand in Naples. A picture tossed by a tempest all over town. When I decided to head back down, I already had an idea for the story I wanted to tell in this book. The idea was that Diego had to die to free the Argentina and Napoli teams, to liberate them at long last from the pressure of relentless scrutiny, the pressure to finally achieve what seemed unachievable, what it seemed that only he, Diego Armando Maradona, World Cup-winner, *campione d'Italia*, could possibly make happen. So far they'd never made it back to the top, not even Messi, whose performance on the pitch was by and large on a par with Diego's, but whose personality could never compare to his compatriot's irresistible persona. Diego's shadow was too big. During the 2022 World Cup, there was a feeling that Argentina could finally cast off that stigma now that Diego was no longer watching.

I entertained a similar notion on my way down to Naples, where I'd be looking for Diego, but well aware that he might be gone, eclipsed by the euphoria over the new stars: Kvaratskhelia, Osimhen et al. And yet the opposite had happened: Diego was more omnipresent than ever, in every store front, on every street. To the point where he's even Photoshopped onto photos of the current team—whose Kvaratskhelia is known as 'Kvaradona'! He's one of them, forever on the team. SSC Napoli's current successes are said to be essentially thanks to him: the myth hasn't faded at all, on the contrary: it looms larger than ever. O Diego, patron saint of Naples!

But this resurrection of the legend had already begun a few years before—probably in the wake of Diego's death in November 2020. Altars were built in the Quartieri Spagnoli and outside the stadium, and Diego could finally become what he'd always been to his devotees: a saint. Because in football, as in the Church, canonisation—in the sense of assessing the degree of heroic virtue in a person's deeds—can only occur posthumously. By this standard of saintliness, there had been no doubt in Naples anyway: he was, after all, the one who'd given them a voice, restored their pride. Football was merely the medium: the sport itself was practically beside the point.

And there, in the midst of all this, was my picture, which had presumably been waiting to find its destiny too. Because if it did once form part of an artistic concept, that was clearly over now. Now it was suddenly popping up in religious processions, Bruno Conti was kneeling down before the icon, and Corrado Ferlaino was bidding farewell to his number 10 at the altar in the Spagnoli. Considerations of the picture's artistic aspects or the function of football

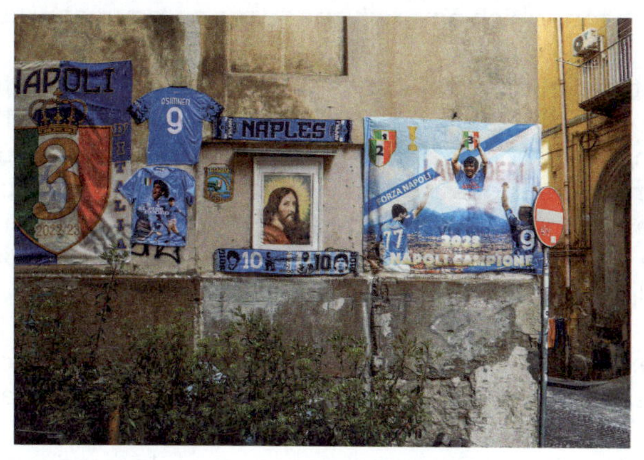

NAPOLI
OSIMHEN
9
NAPLES
3
2022/23
FORZA NAPOLI
77
2023
NAPOLI CAMPIONE
9

in modern secular society no longer figured here. These were religious acts in real time.

I won't deny that I had mixed feelings about all this. I was primarily fascinated that anything like this could happen at all: that, through no effort on my part, my work should suddenly find itself centre-stage in another land—and in this particular place and context as well. Naturally, it's gratifying to see my picture hailed as an appropriate and authentic image. Not only is it an icon, but it has now come to be revered as such too, which naturally made me somewhat proud.

But my positive reactions were soured by an awfully uncomfortable feeling. What had become of the tongue-in-cheek subtext? Why was everything suddenly so serious? Where was the critical distance? Was this still art? My creation was now taking on a life of its own—and getting out of control. I couldn't help thinking of Frankenstein: 'It's alive!'

Hence my ambivalence. When I put an image out there in the world, there's no way of planning what'll happen with it in the end. And that's a good thing. That's what really interests me: multi-layered ambiguity that allows for a multiplicity of perspectives. This is what my work has always been about—likewise my idea of portraying footballers as saints: to create cultural artefacts that resonate on very different levels and allow for contrasting narratives in dissimilar contexts. In retrospect, I'd say they've succeeded in doing precisely that.

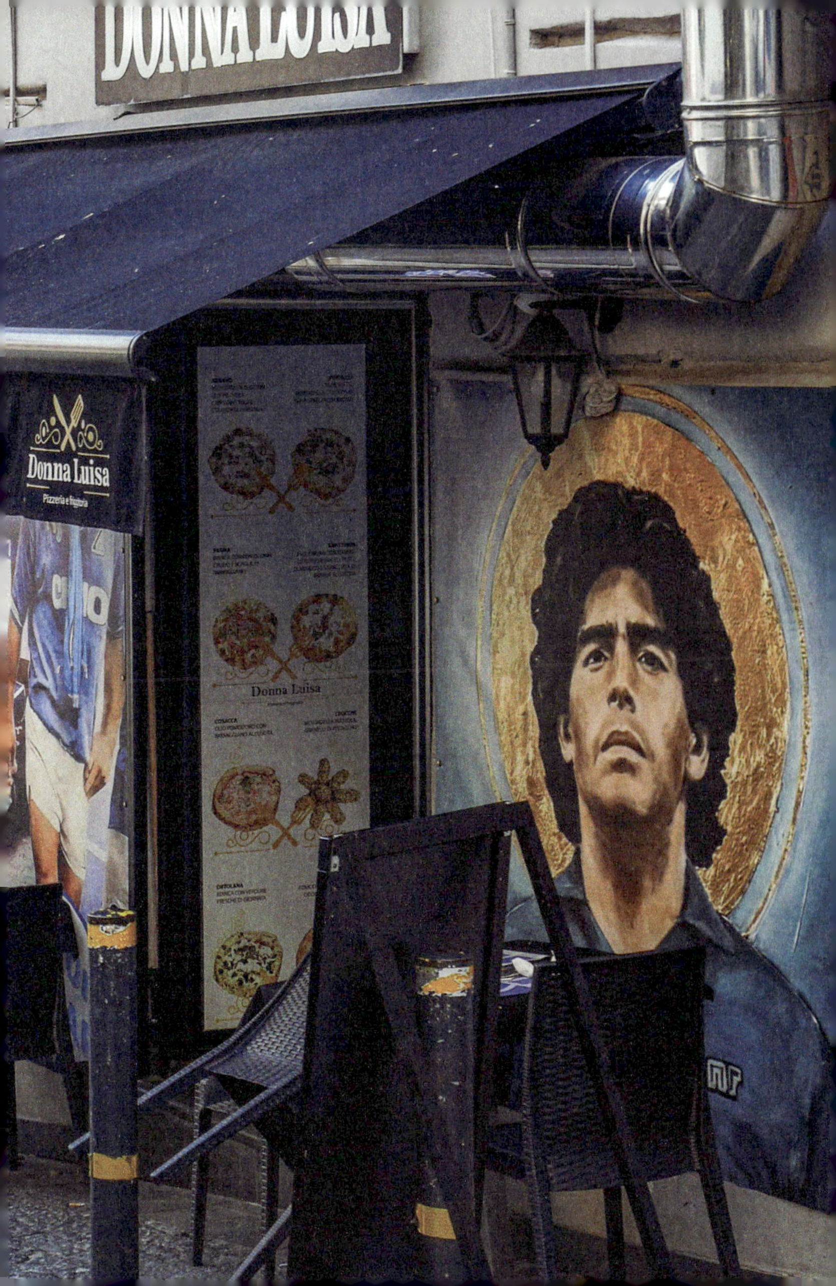

DONNA LUISA
Donna Luisa
Pizzeria e Rosticceria
Donna Luisa

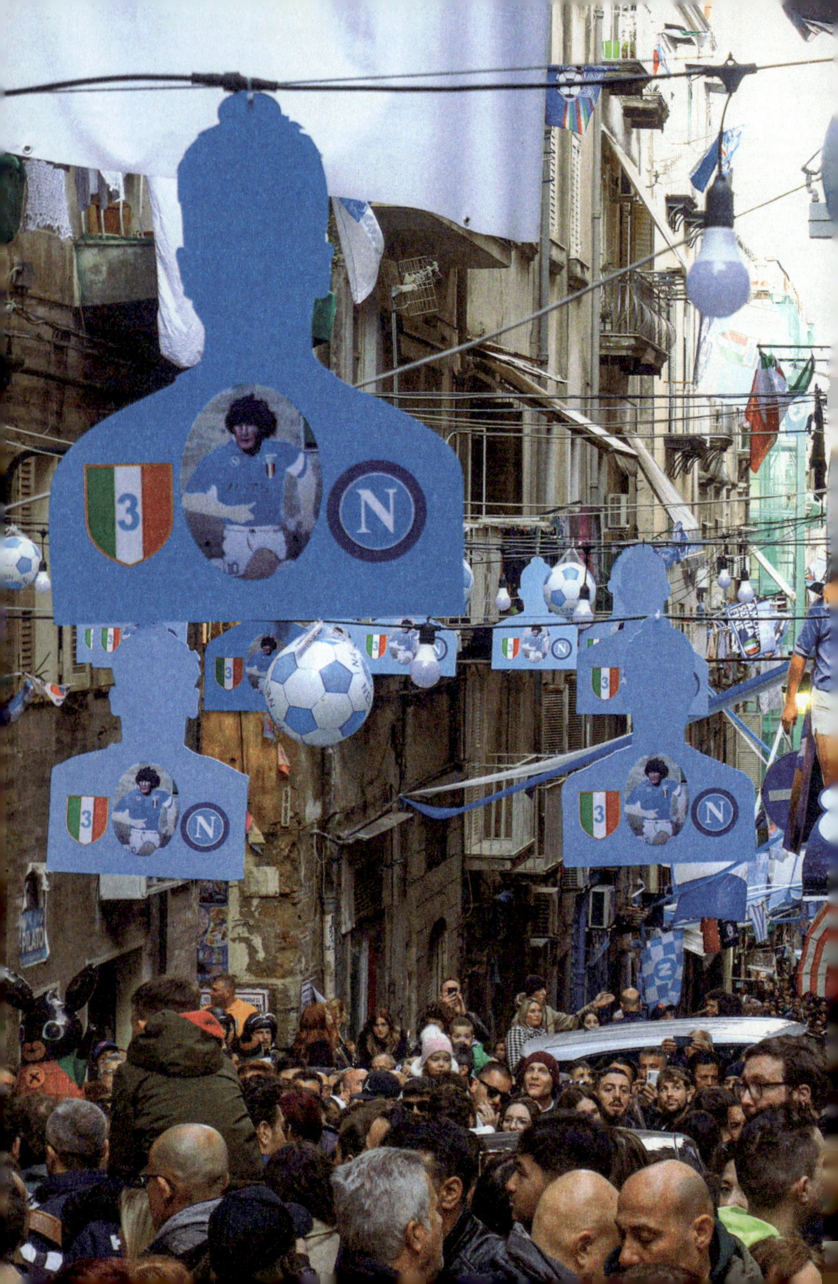

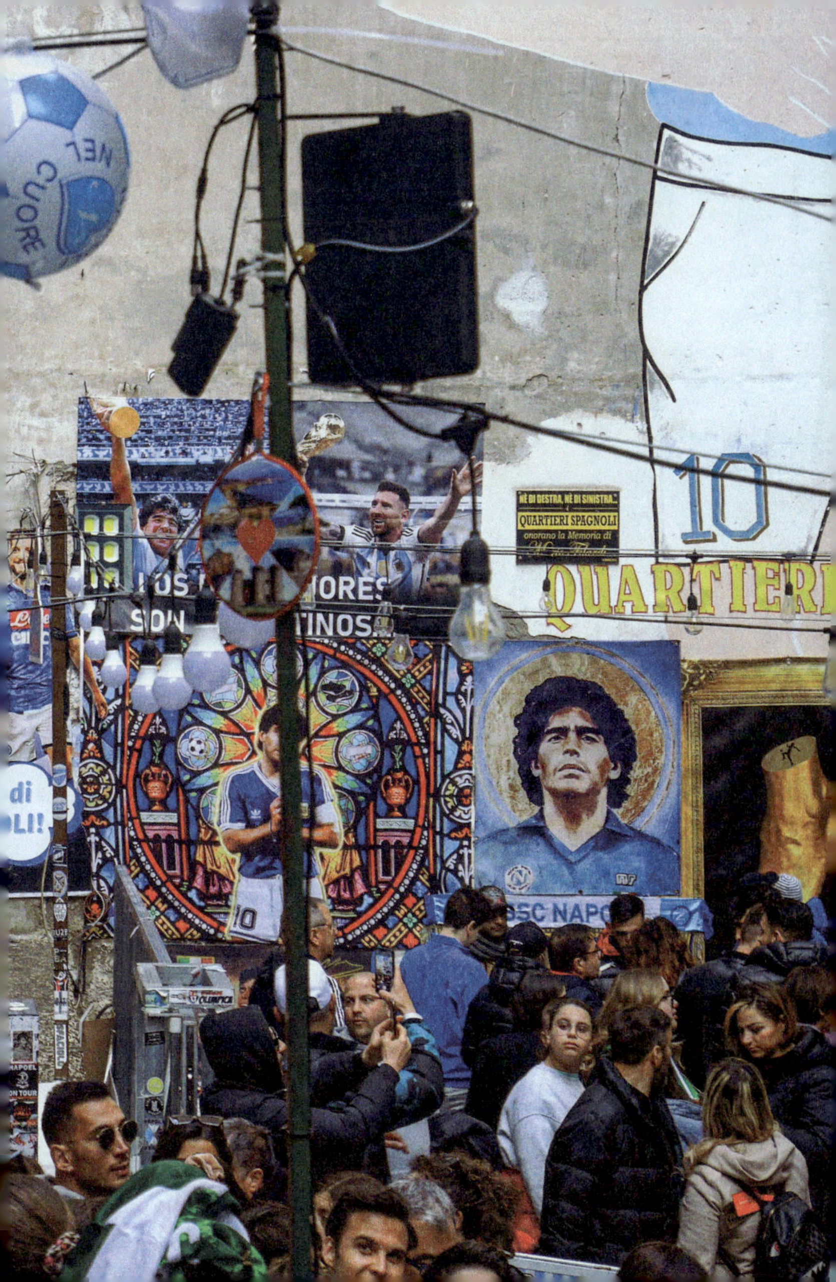

NEL CUORE
NÈ DI DESTRA, NÈ DI SINISTRA...
QUARTIERI SPAGNOLI
onorano la Memoria di
10
QUARTIERI
LOS ... ORES
SON ...TINOS
SSC NAPOLI
di
OLI!
OLIMPICA

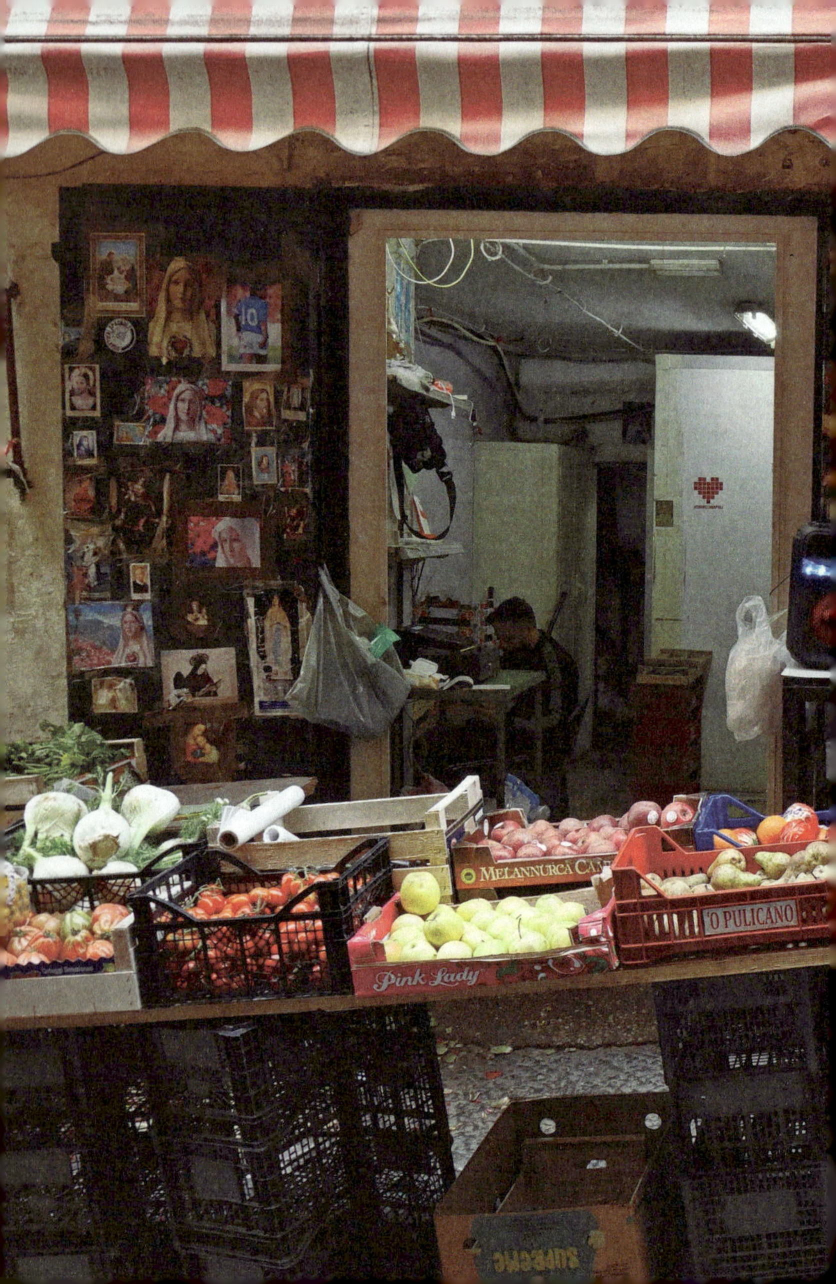

10
MELANNURCA CA...
'O PULICANO
Pink Lady

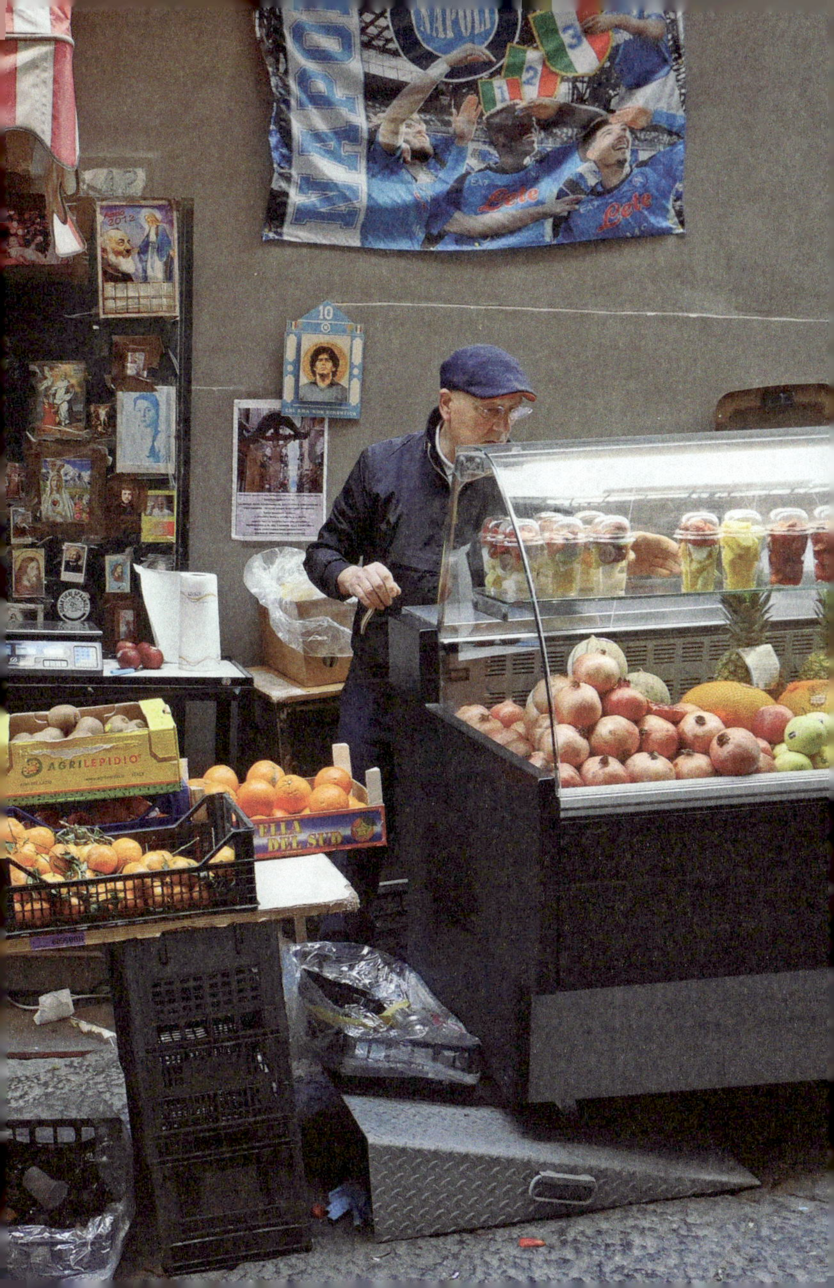

NAPOLI
1 2 3
Lete
Lete
10
CHI AMA NON DIMENTICA
AGRILEPIDIO
ITALY
ELLA DEL SUD

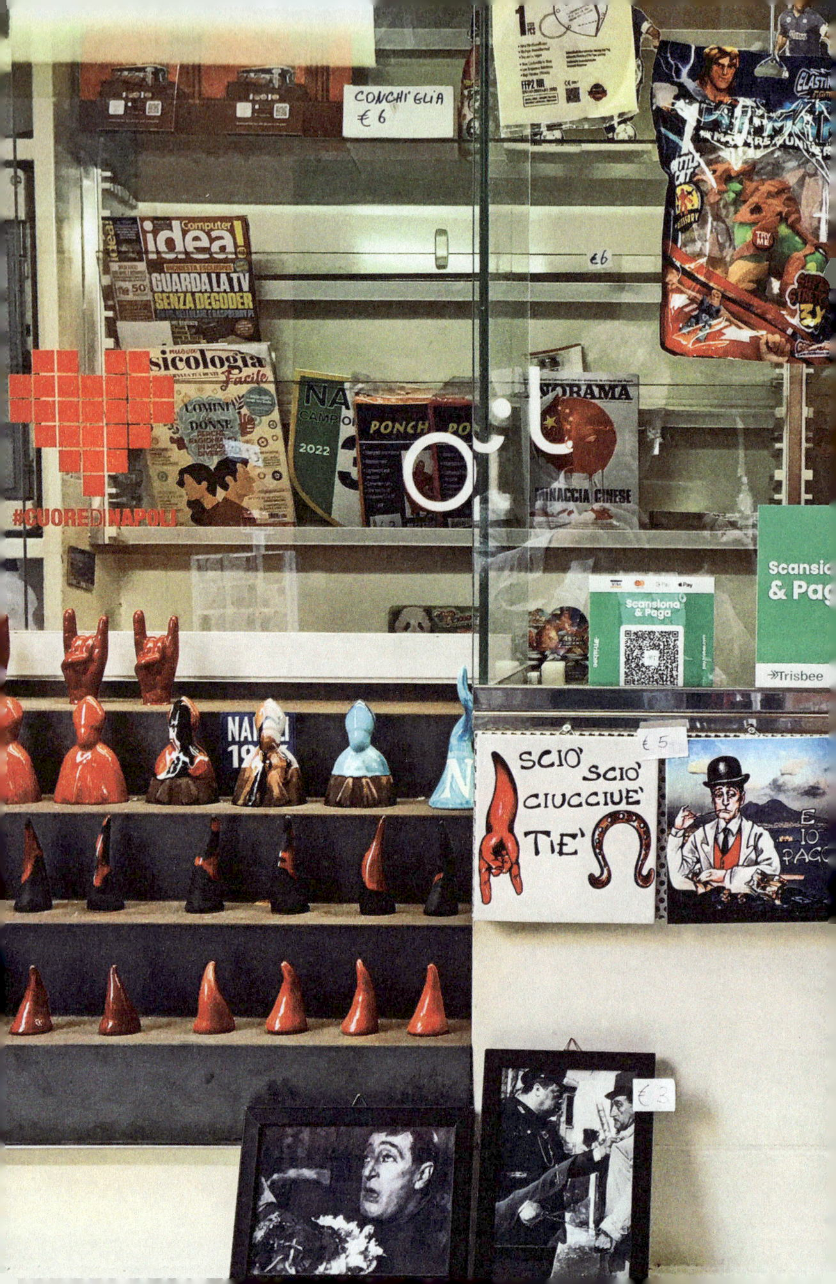

CONCHIGLIA
€ 6
Computer
idea!
GUARDA LA TV
SENZA DECODER
sicologia
Facile
DONNE
PONCH
ORAMA
MINACCIA CINESE
#CUOREDINAPOLI
NAPOLI
1926
Scansiona
& Paga
Trisbee
€ 5
SCIO' SCIO'
CIUCCIUE'
TIE'
E IO
PAGO
€ 3

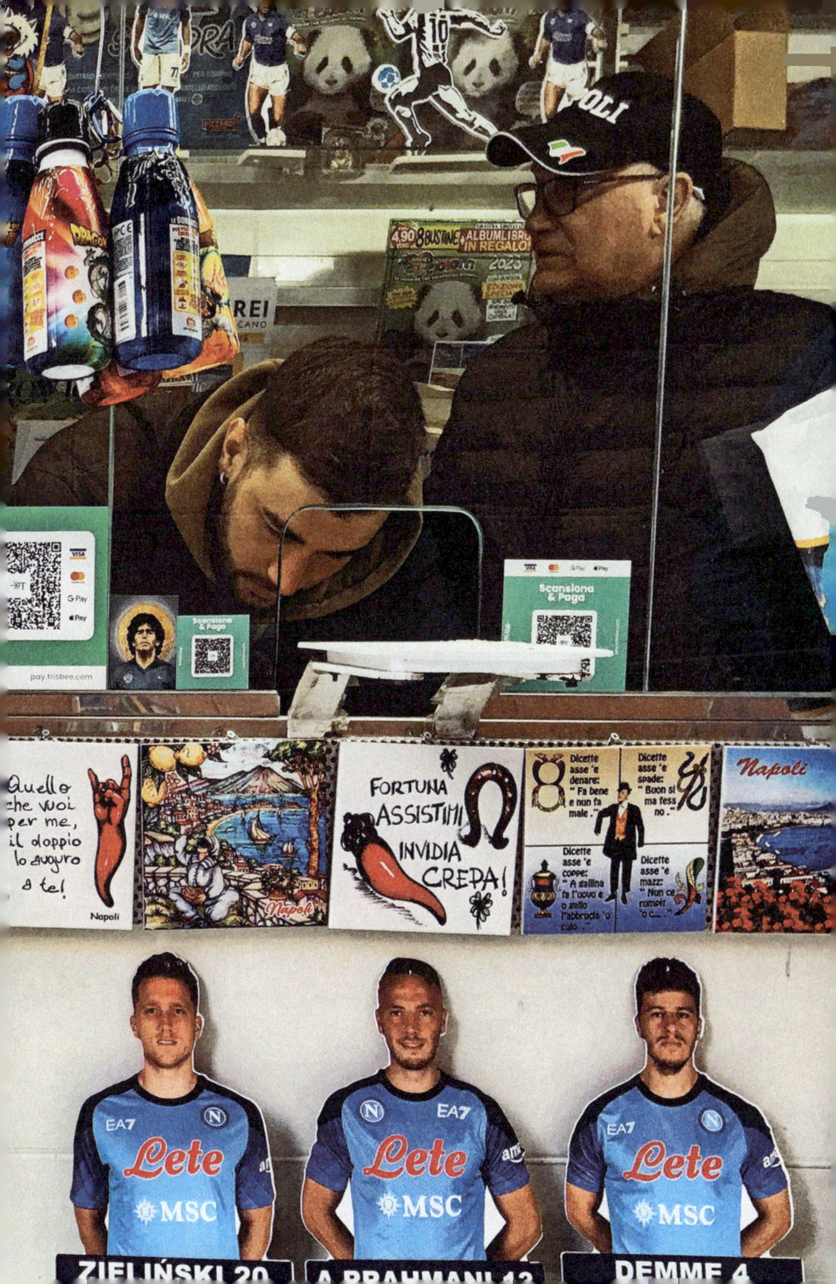
Quello
che vuoi
per me,
il doppio
lo auguro
a te!
Napoli
FORTUNA
ASSISTIMI
INVIDIA
CREPA!
Dicette
asse 'e
denare:
"Fa bene
e nun fa
male."
Dicette
asse 'e
spade:
"Buon sì
ma fess
no."
Dicette
asse 'e
coppe:
"A gallina
fa l'uovo e
o gallo
l'abbrucia 'o
culo."
Dicette
asse 'e
mazz:
"Nun ce
rumpit
'o c..."
Napoli
Scansiona
& Paga
Scansiona
& Paga
pay.trisbee.com
ZIELIŃSKI 20
A BRAHMANI 12
DEMME 4

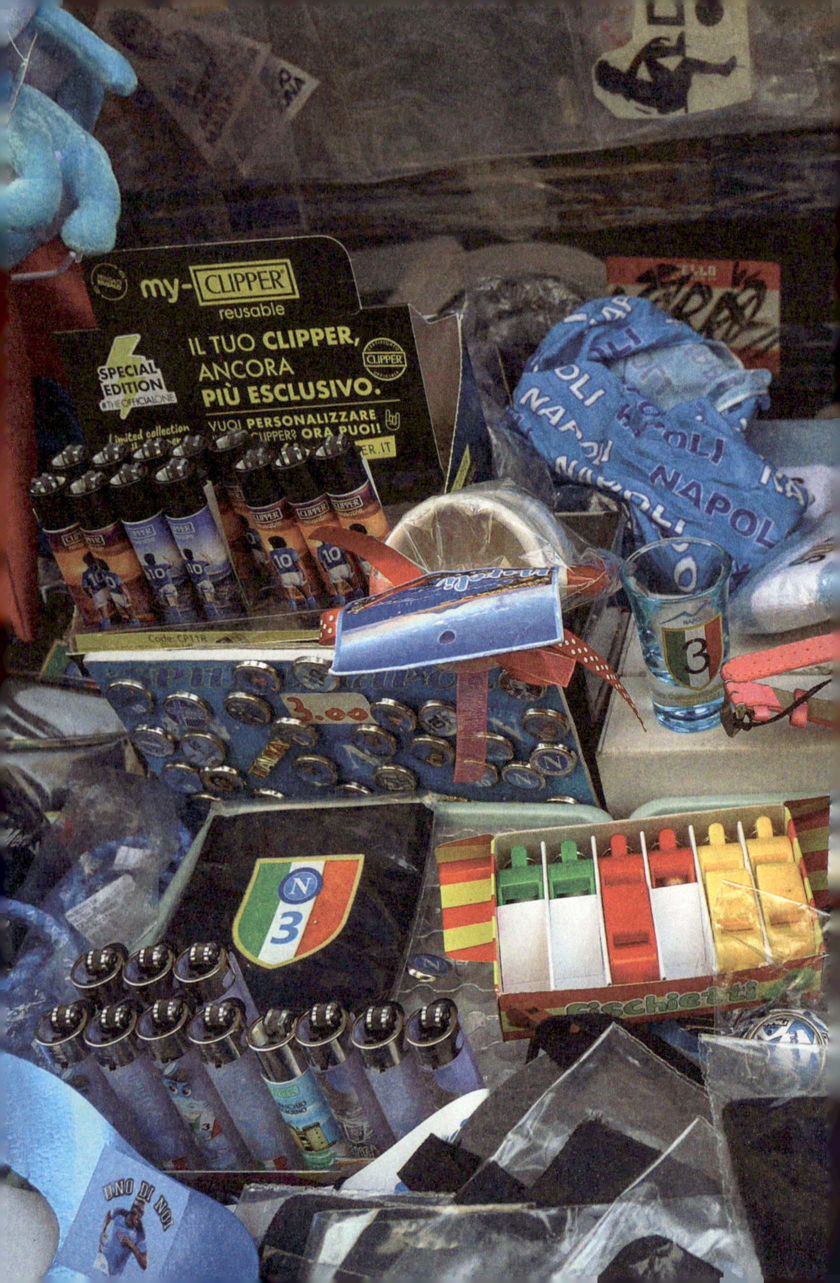

my-CLIPPER
reusable
IL TUO CLIPPER,
ANCORA
PIÙ ESCLUSIVO.
SPECIAL
EDITION
#THEOFFICIALONE
limited collection
VUOI PERSONALIZZARE
IL CLIPPER? ORA PUOI!
CLIPPER.IT
10
Code: CP11R
3.00
NAPOLI
NAPOLI
NAPOL
N
3
fischietti
UNO DI NOI

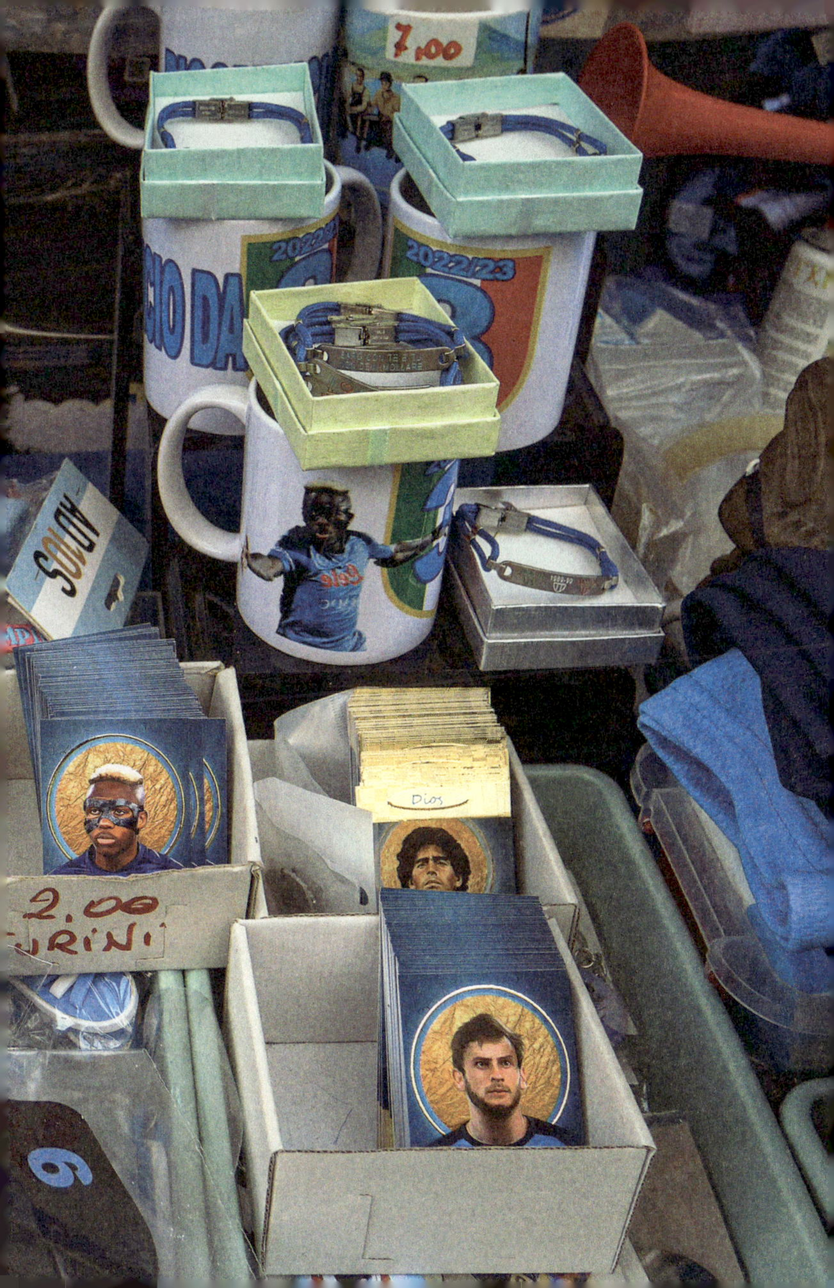

7,00
2022/23
2022/23
SOLO
2,00
URINI
Dios
9

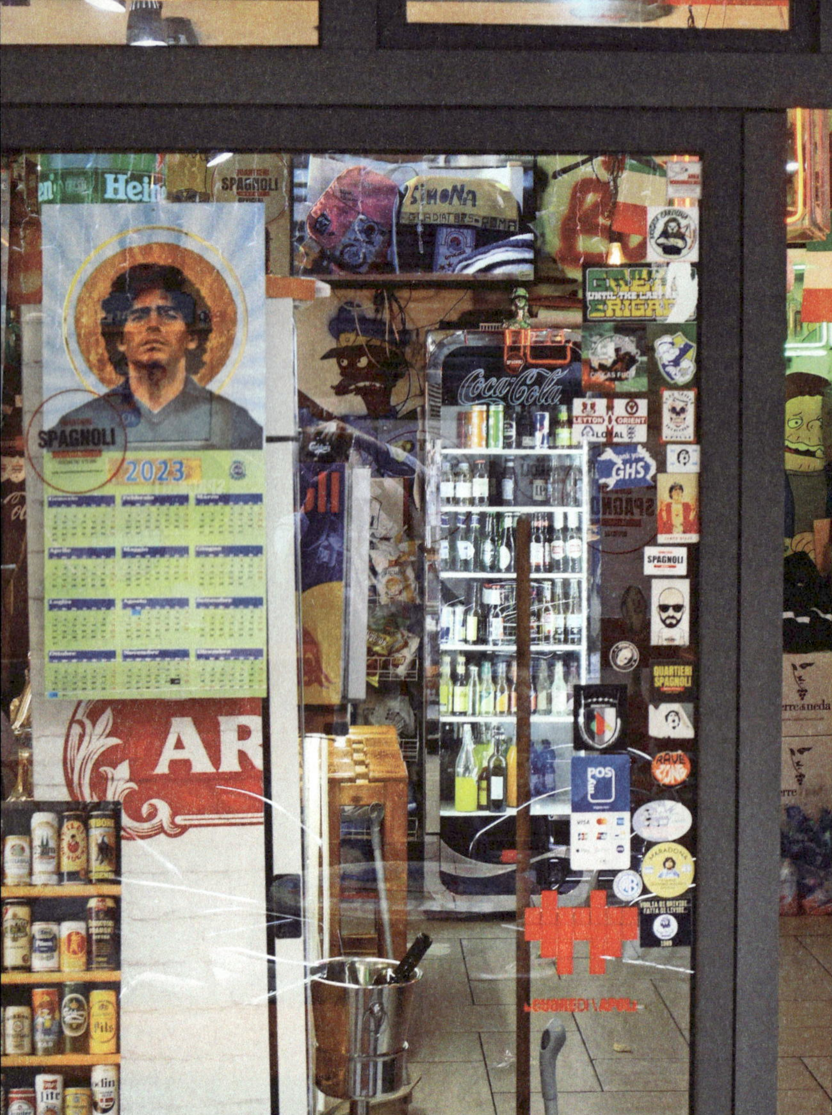

Hei
SPAGNOLI
SiMoNA
GLADIATORS ROMA
UNTIL THE LAST
BRIGA
Coca-Cola
LEYTON ORIENT
LOCAL
GHS
SPAGNO
SPAGNOLI
QUARTIERI
SPAGNOLI
POS
VISA
RAVE
MARADONA
2023
SPAGNOLI
AR

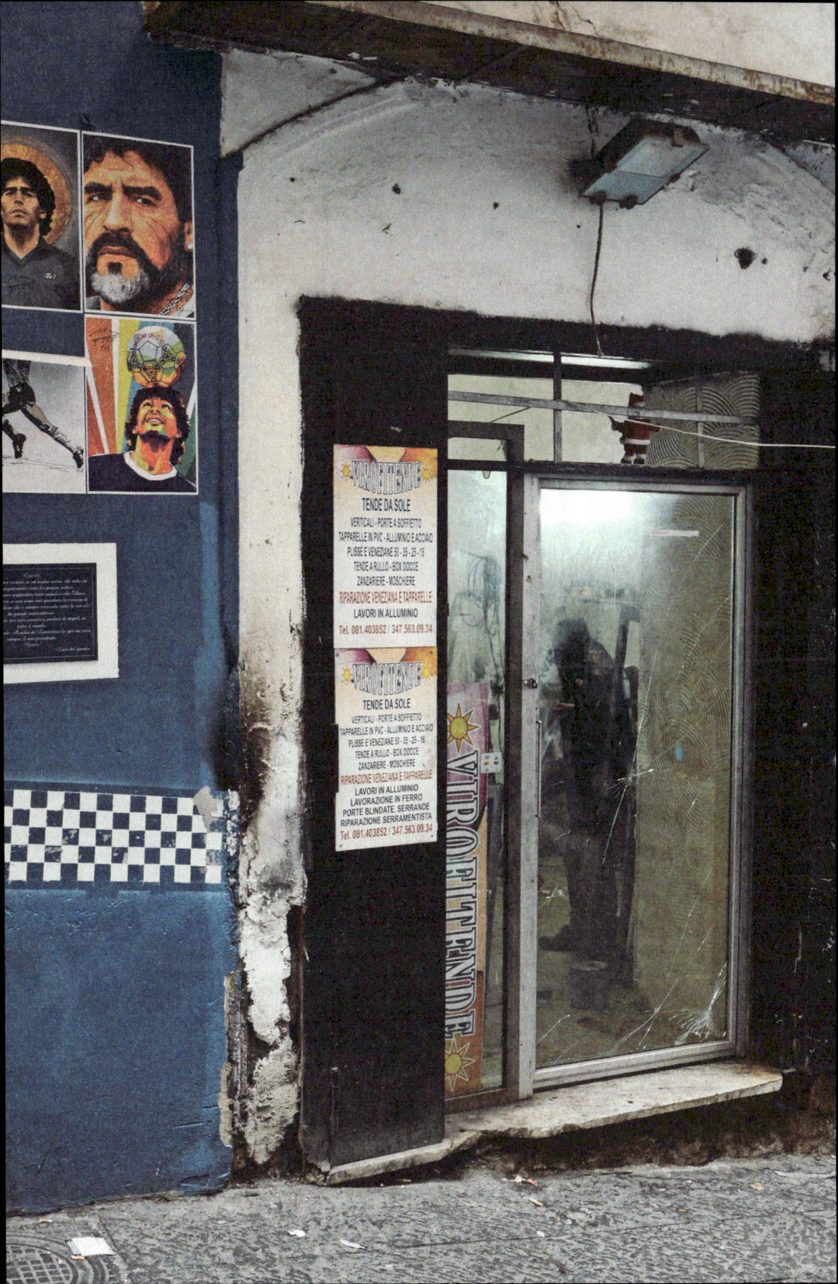
VIROFITENDE
TENDE DA SOLE
VERTICALI - PORTE A SOFFIETTO
TAPPARELLE IN PVC - ALLUMINIO E ACCIAIO
PLISSE E VENEZIANE 50 - 35 - 25 - 16
TENDE A RULLO - BOX DOCCE
ZANZARIERE - MOSCHIERE
RIPARAZIONE VENEZIANA E TAPPARELLE
LAVORI IN ALLUMINIO
Tel. 081.403852 / 347.563.09.34
VIROFITENDE
TENDE DA SOLE
VERTICALI - PORTE A SOFFIETTO
TAPPARELLE IN PVC - ALLUMINIO E ACCIAIO
PLISSE E VENEZIANE 50 - 35 - 16
TENDE A RULLO - BOX DOCCE
ZANZARIERE - MOSCHIERE
RIPARAZIONE VENEZIANA E TAPPARELLE
LAVORI IN ALLUMINIO
LAVORAZIONE IN FERRO
PORTE BLINDATE, SERRANDE
RIPARAZIONE SERRAMENTISTA
Tel. 081.403852 / 347.563.09.34
VIROFITENDE

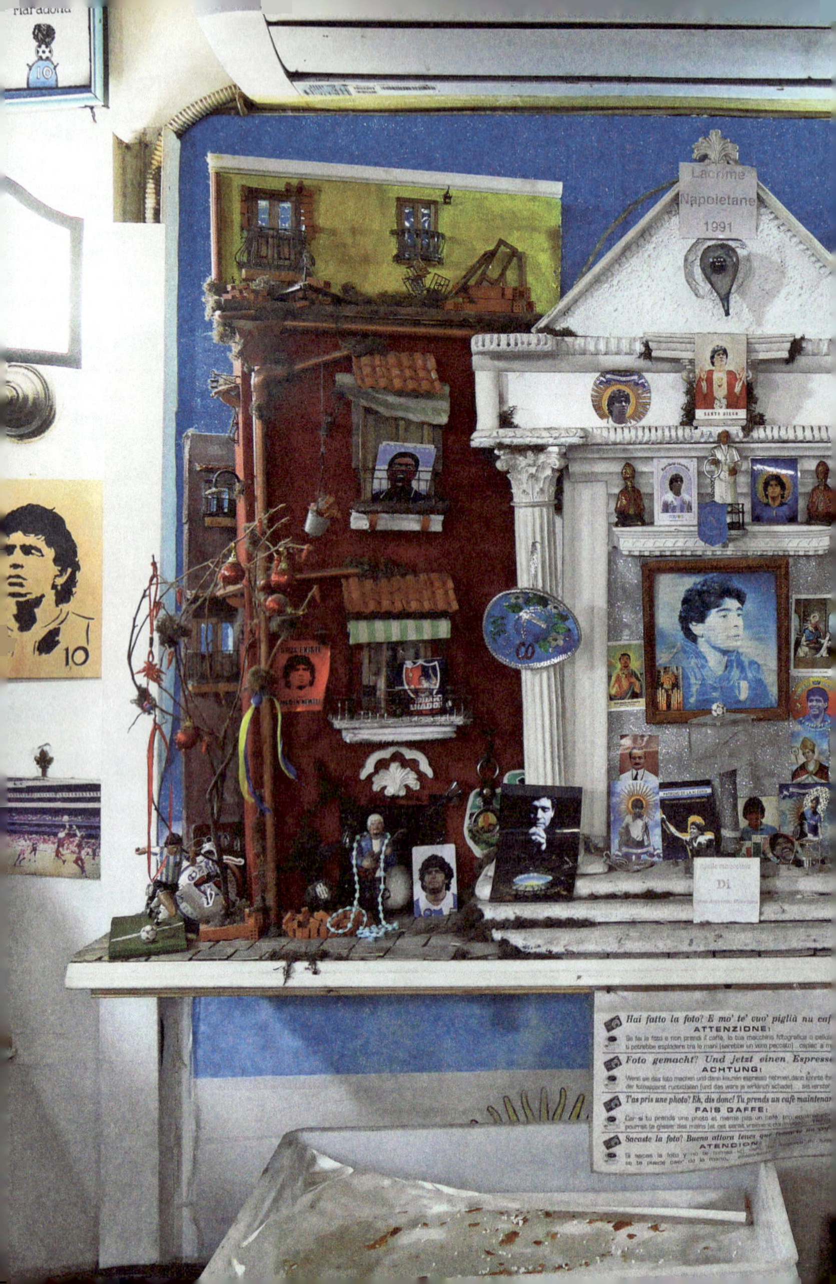

Maradona
10
Lacrime
Napoletane
1991
SANTO DIEGO
10

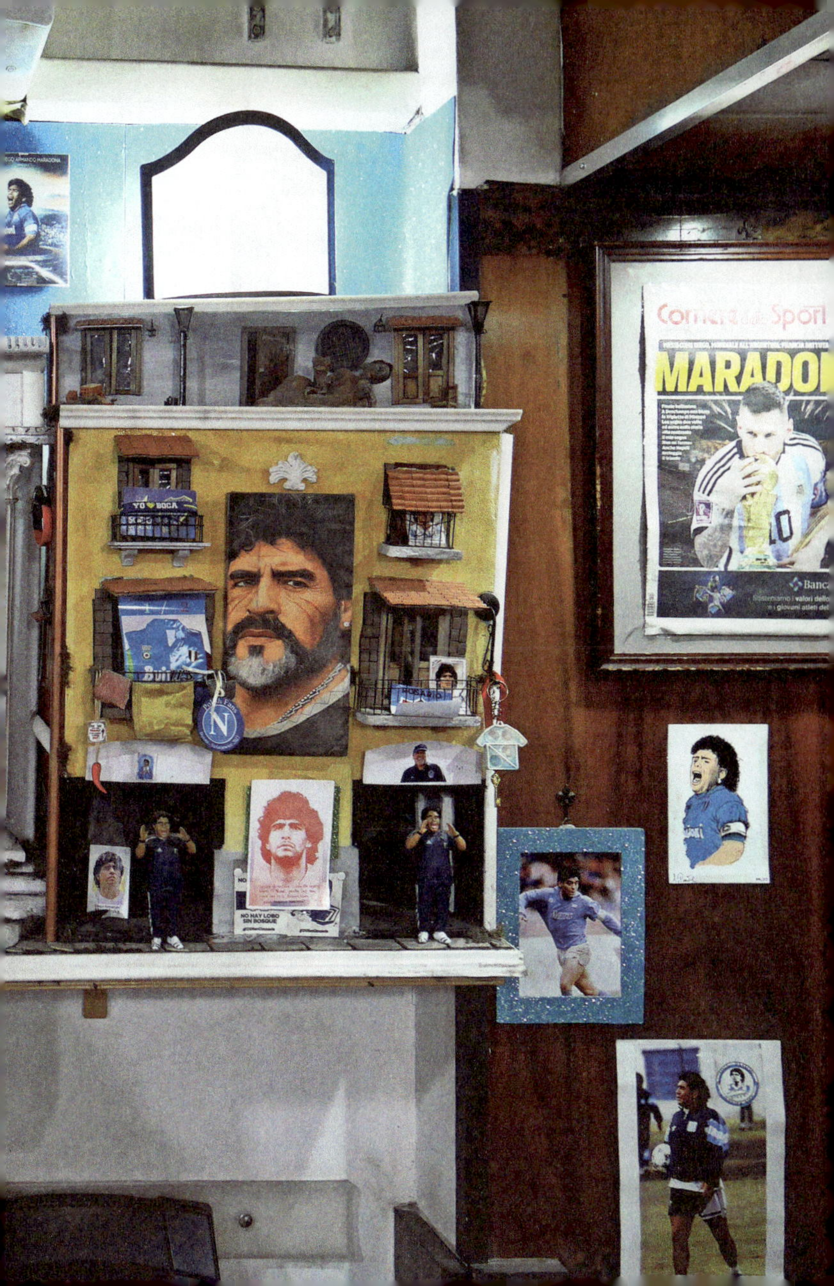
Corriere dello Sport
MARADON
YO ♥ BOCA
ROSARIO
NO HAY LOBO
SIN BOSQUE

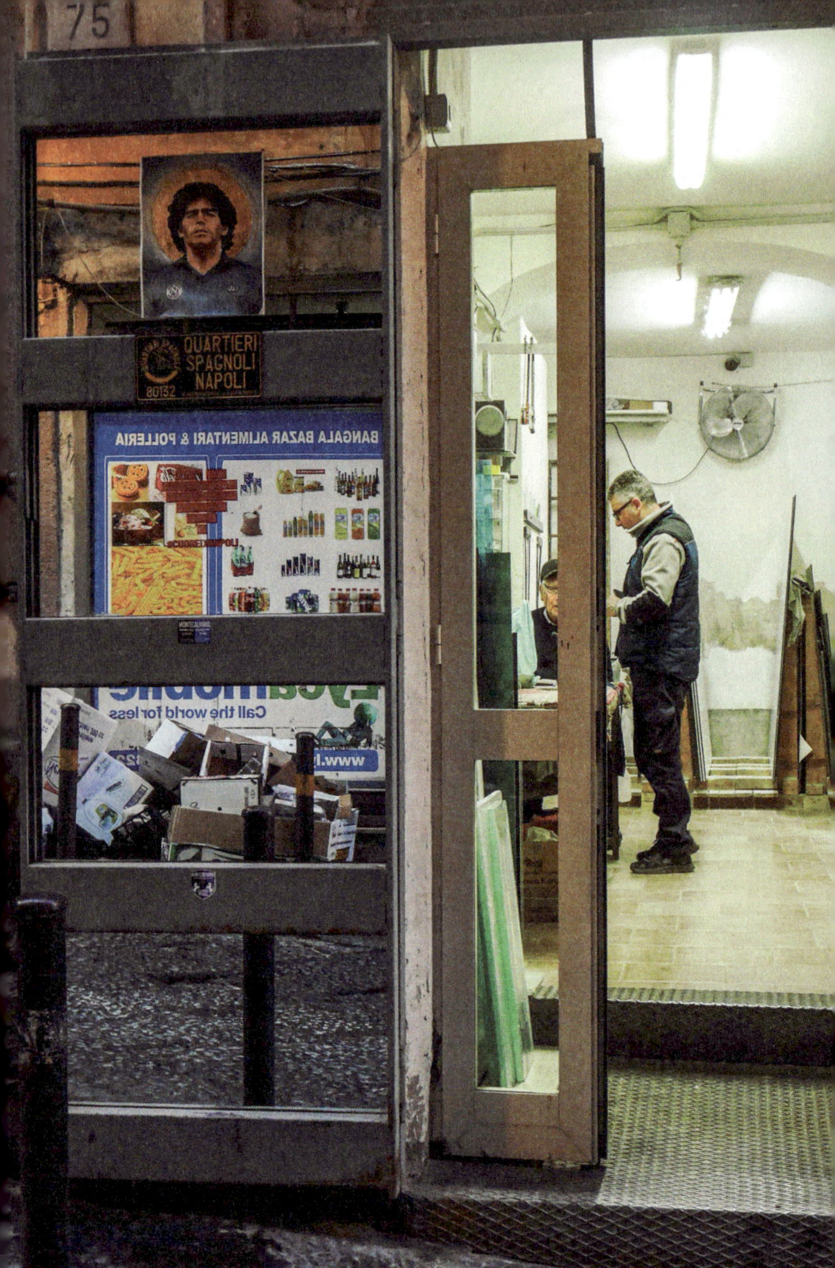

75
QUARTIERI SPAGNOLI NAPOLI
80132
BANGALA BAZAR ALIMENTARI & POLLERIA
Call the world for less
www.

Paintings by David Diehl
Notes by Mämä Sykora

Part II

When the slight lad with the unsteady look crept across the pitch, he was all but invisible. And yet, when the ball kissed his foot, the whole stadium witnessed the most wondrous symbiosis. Foot and ball fused into a single organism that was too fast for the others, and when they tried to seize it, it eluded them like sand running through their fingers. Afterwards, they couldn't fathom how the ball had suddenly, in the blink of an eye, landed in the net, and could only look on as he turned back into the slight boy he'd been before. Until the next kiss.

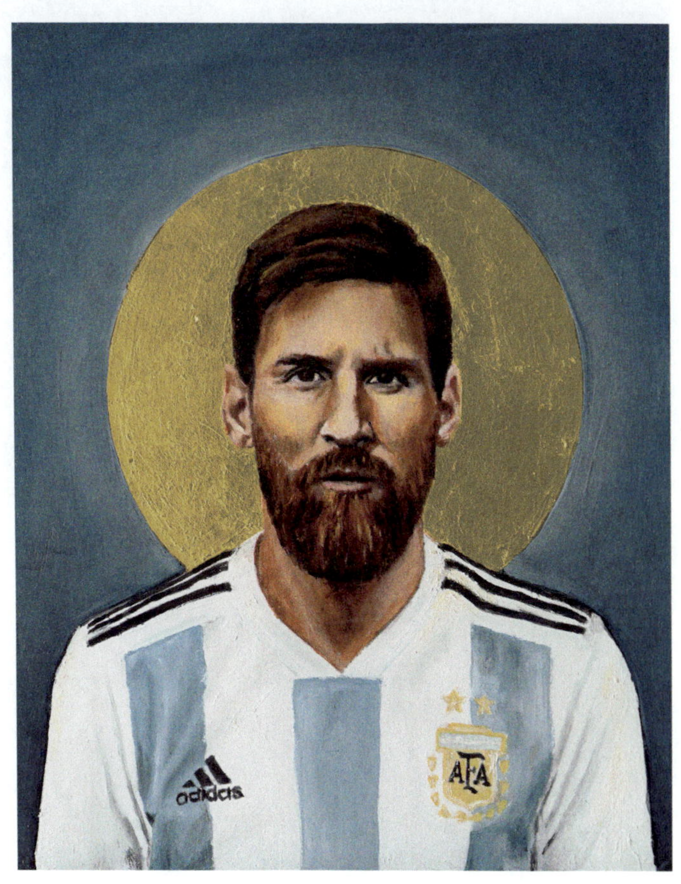

Lionel Messi

Talent is the oxygen that fuels many a footballer. But he knows that air is mostly made up of nitrogen, and his nitrogen is ambition. While others are still revelling in their latest victories, he's already hard at work again, lifting weights, or fine-tuning his striking and sprinting technique. Until his body has become so perfect for the beautiful game that any sculptor's attempts to render it are doomed to pitiful failure. His opponents bounce up and down beside his lofty leaps. And by the time they start running down field, he's already long since left them in the dust.

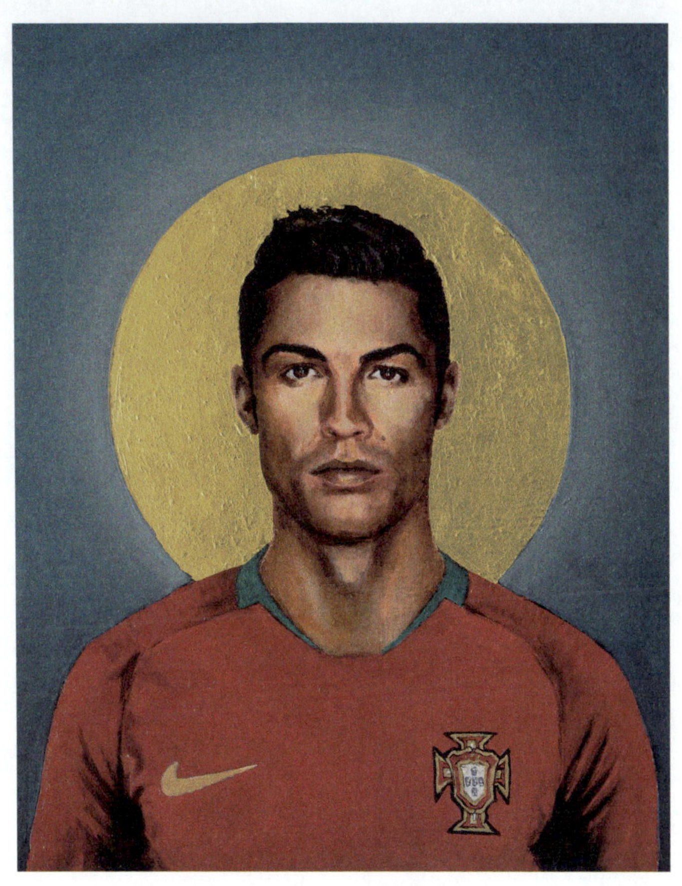

Cristiano Ronaldo

Why, everyone asks him, why don't you finally pack
it in? You know every podium like the back of your
hand, you've got so many trophies and awards you
don't know what to do with them all. You've seen it all.
You've vanquished them all. People go into raptures
at the mere mention of your name. So why don't you
just help yourself to a glass of wine and some well-
earned R&R? He just smiles, velcroes up his gloves
and gets back in the goal.

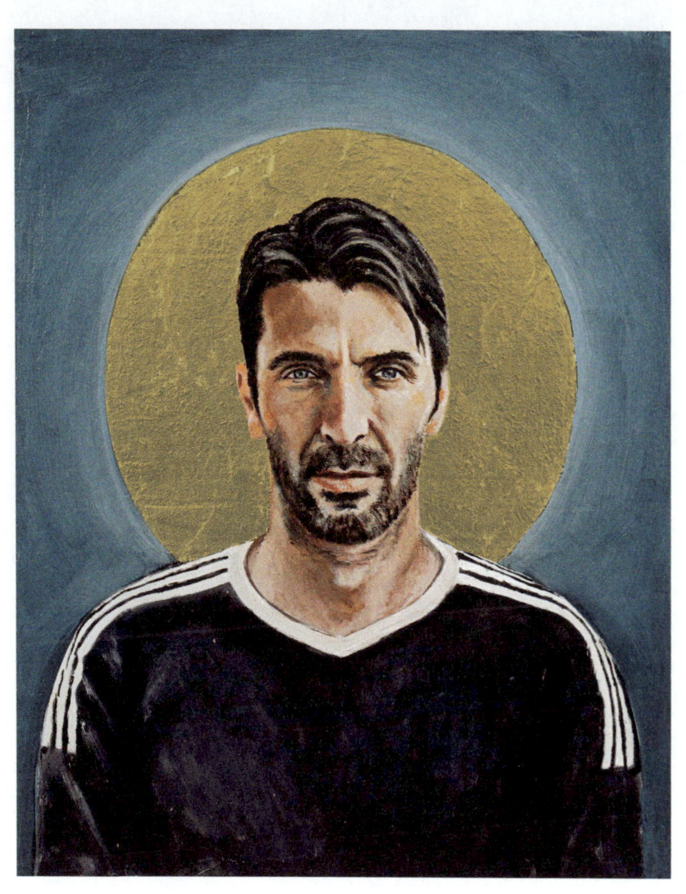

Gianluigi Buffon

'*Presto e bene non vanno insieme*,' they say in Italy: fast and good don't go together. So he'd amble through the midfield, keeping the ball at his feet like a *cameriere* with an *espresso macchiato* on a tray winds his way through rows of tables at a poky outdoor Milanese *caffè*. He doesn't bump into anyone or anything, the liquid in the cup remains unrippled, obstacles don't exist for him: perfect service with pinpoint precision.

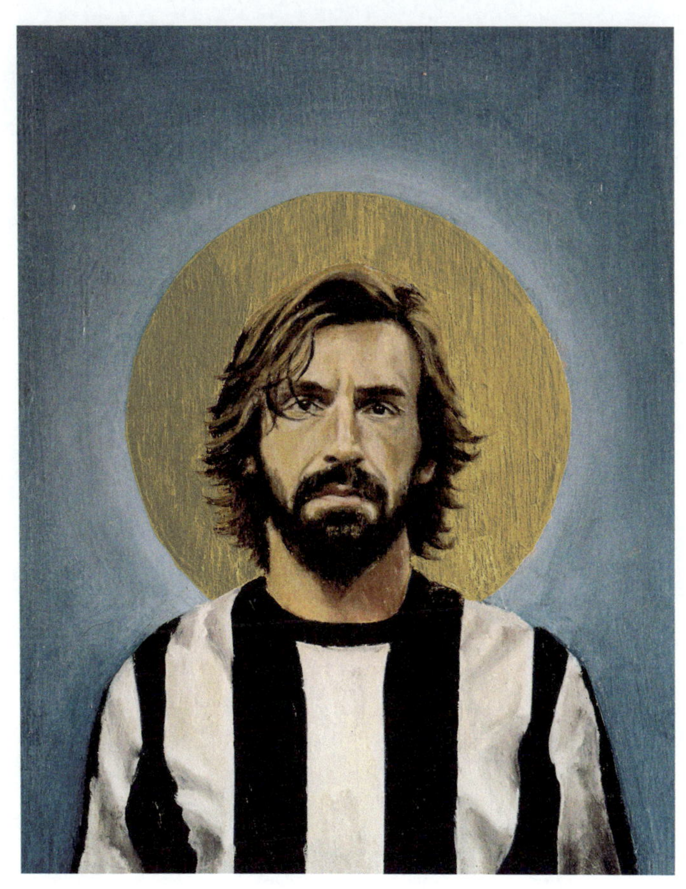

Andrea Pirlo

He was everywhere and yet scarcely visible. While others were basking in the sunshine of fame, he was making a clean sweep of any threats in the shade. He was servant, henchman, protector and soldier. Hardly anyone even took notice of him because the king eclipsed everyone, and yet without him there'd never have been a king in the first place.

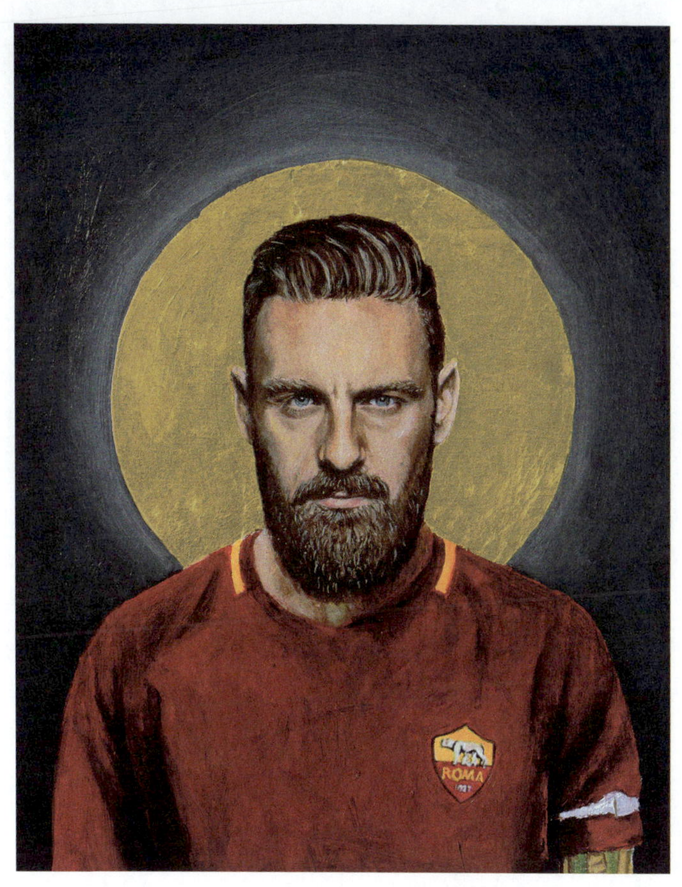

Daniele De Rossi

The whole red machine grinds to a halt on the spot without him, its little engine. Without a flicker of emotion, he intercepts passes, performs a *croqueta*, flicking the ball from his right foot to his left, then turns the pitch into a canvas upon which to trace the lines and arcs of football history. His nation had pinned their hopes on the team's showboats and bigmouths for so long—in vain. But when, after dozens of dashed dreams, they made the grade at long last, the final goal was scored by him, of course, the incredible wallflower in midfield.

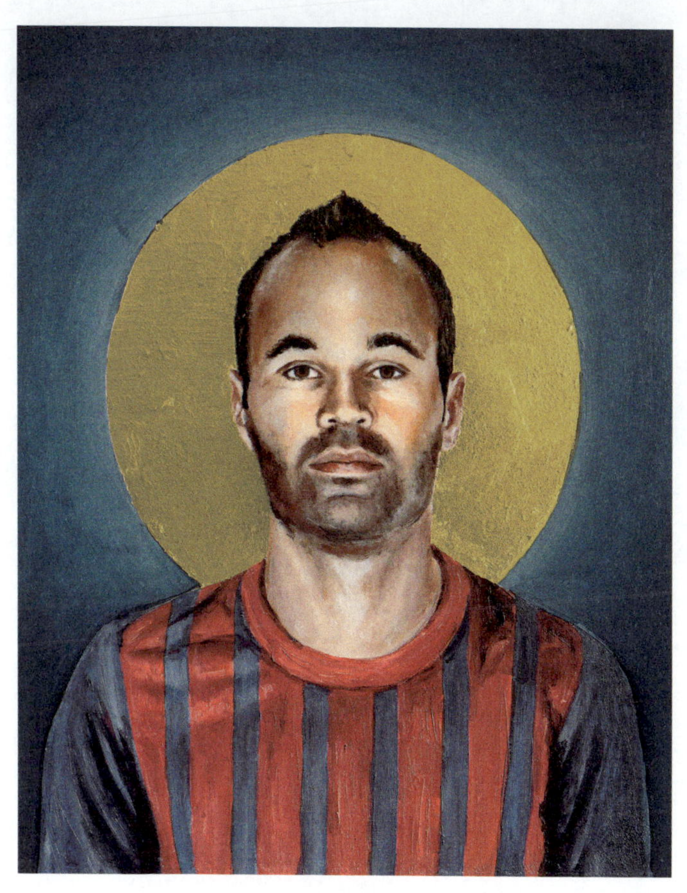

Andrés Iniesta

The curse is lodged in just a few square inches of pitch. Which is precisely where the ball finds Gerrard. But this time his foot, venerated for its sure-fire reliability, slips and down he goes. A mere split second, but long enough for his life's dream to slip away with it as he looks helplessly on. What has he done to deserve this cruel punishment? Who would begrudge him this one long-awaited triumph? There is no answer to this conundrum.

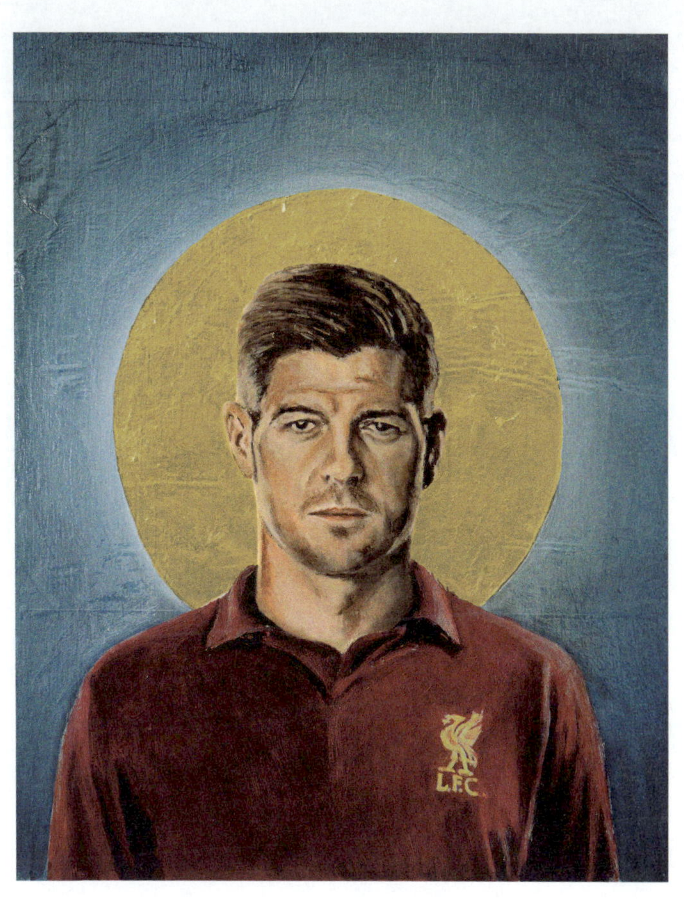

Steven Gerrard

It was drilled into them a hundred times: Stand him up or he'll whizz past you like a cannonball! And they kept on him with stern discipline. Guarded by four defenders, with his back to goal, even he couldn't do any damage, surely … But, when a pass comes over to him, he flicks the ball knee-high, spins on his heels and lofts it over the heads of defenders and keeper and into the back of the net.

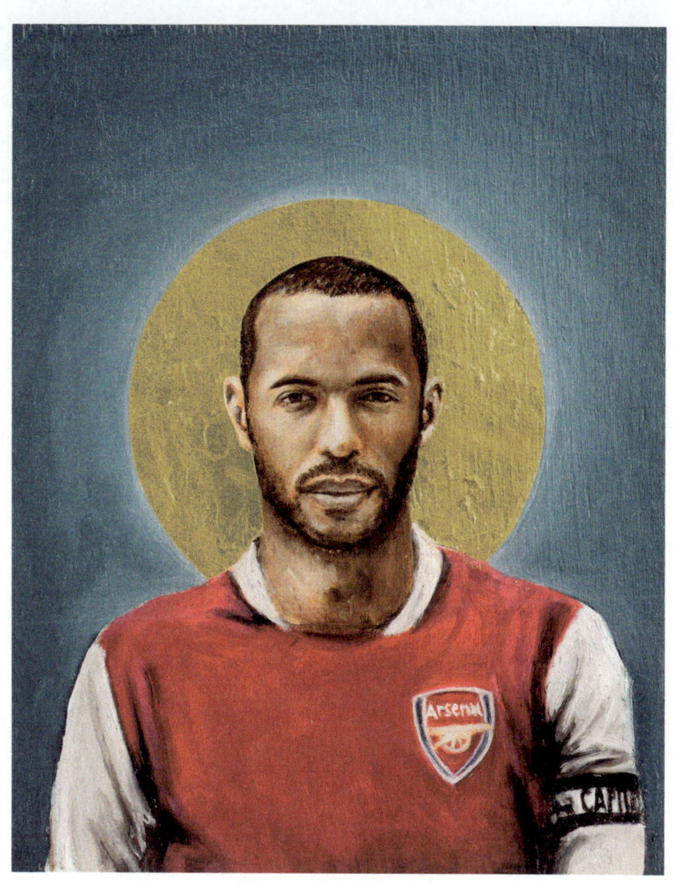

Thierry Henry

1966 was a good year for England, says the billboard. After all, that's when he was born. He is the foreigner who reduces the natives to dimwitted stooges as he weaves his way around them before putting more feeling into a lob than the island has seen in a hundred years of football. His fans cover their open mouths in disbelief, whilst the opposing fans are incensed at this reminder that none of their own will ever play with such surefooted nonchalance.

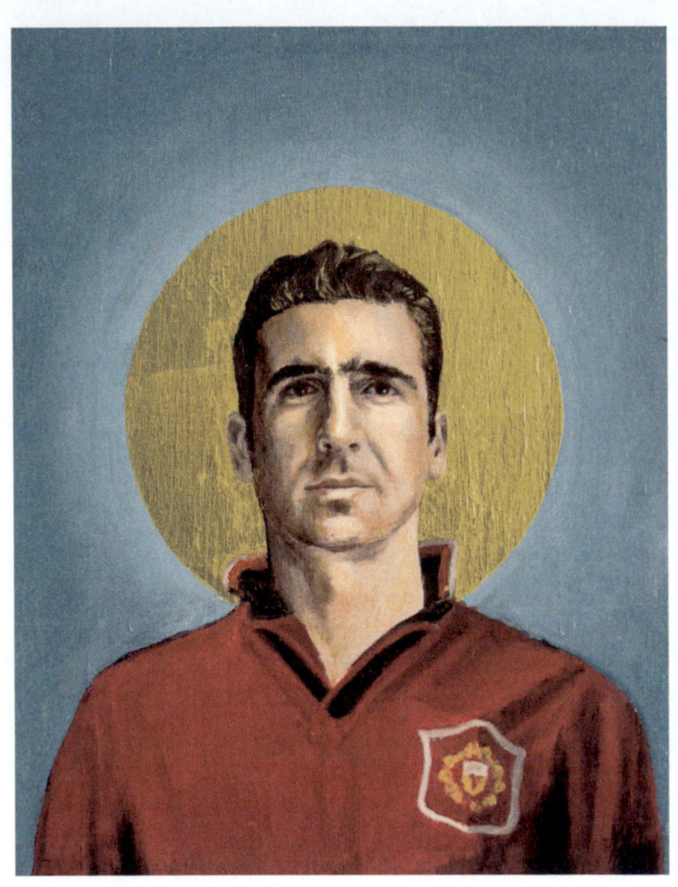

Éric Cantona

A dash, a leap, upside-down in the air, a twist and then the landing. His sister might have looked more elegant executing this somersault at the Olympic Games. But the masses went into raptures at this acrobatic display, because it meant he'd scored yet again. As he almost always did.

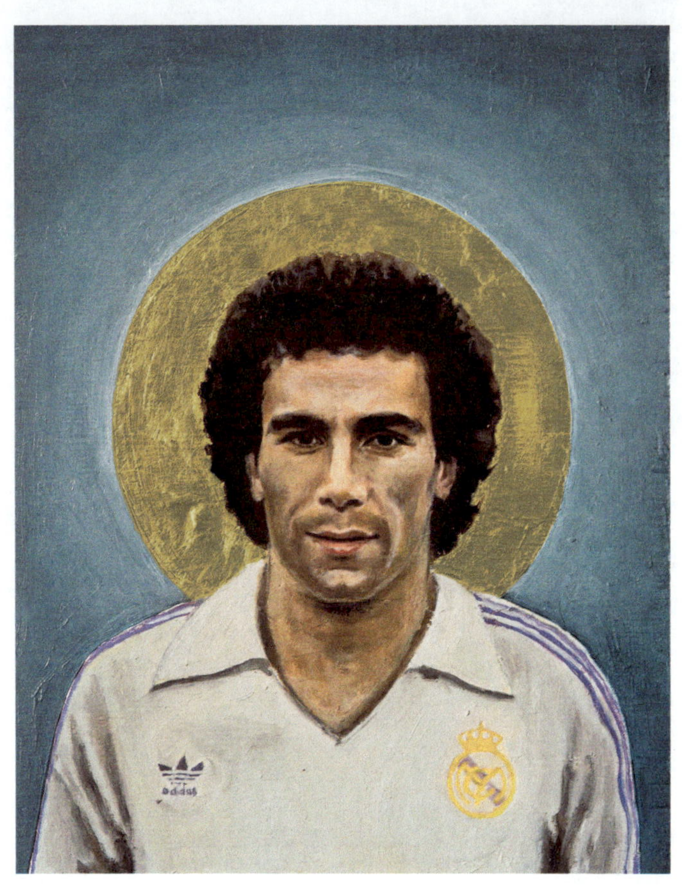

Hugo Sánchez

When players go out of their way to taunt or pro-
voke their opponents or blithely bend the rules, it
really rubs most spectators the wrong way. Not so
in Argentina, however. They call it *picardía*, and nod
their heads appreciatively. The uncontested master
of this 'discipline', he was demonised around the
world for it—and lionised in his native land.

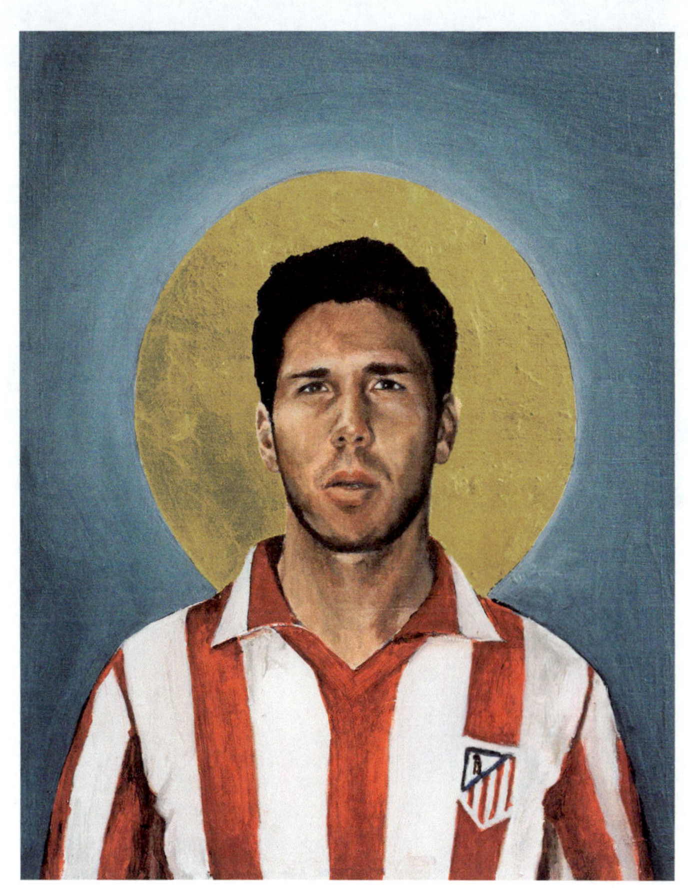

Diego Simeone

He sets off from his own penalty box with strides long enough to clear whole rivers. He overtakes his opponents so fast that their yellow jerseys blur before his eyes; darting right, then left, he dribbles straight through three defenders. They push, pull and kick away at him, but all to no avail: there's no stopping this force of nature, though so many have tried. One of them once stuck an outstretched boot into his massive thigh, and a stud broke off on impact. He didn't even falter.

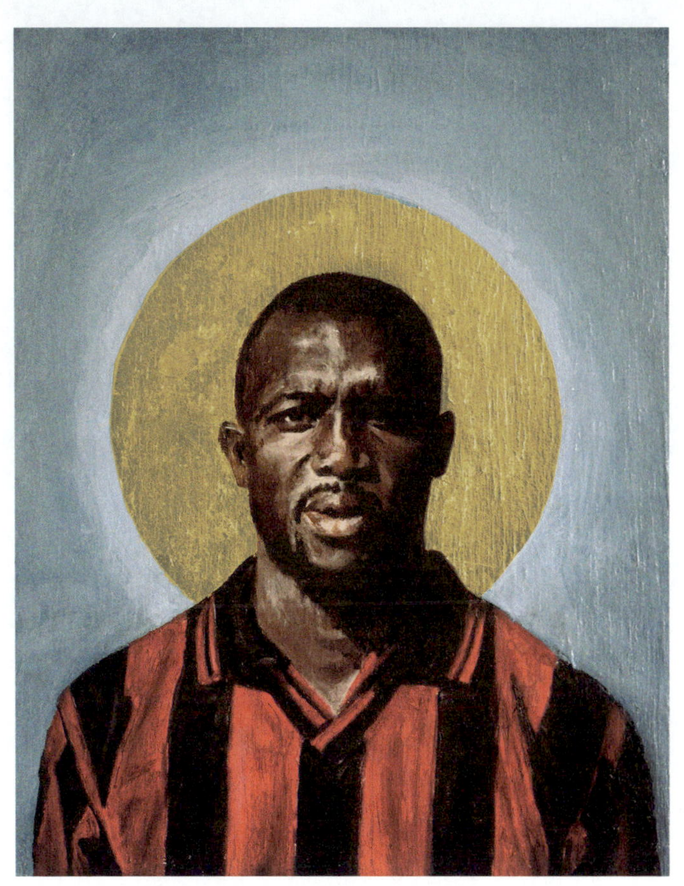

George Weah

Thirty thousand, seven hundred minutes. That's how much time he spent running up and down the pitch, dodging defenders, scoring with his left foot or his right, with his head, from the goalmouth scramble or from distance, cheering, being cheered or consoled. And never, not once in all those 30,700 minutes, did he run afoul of the man in black.

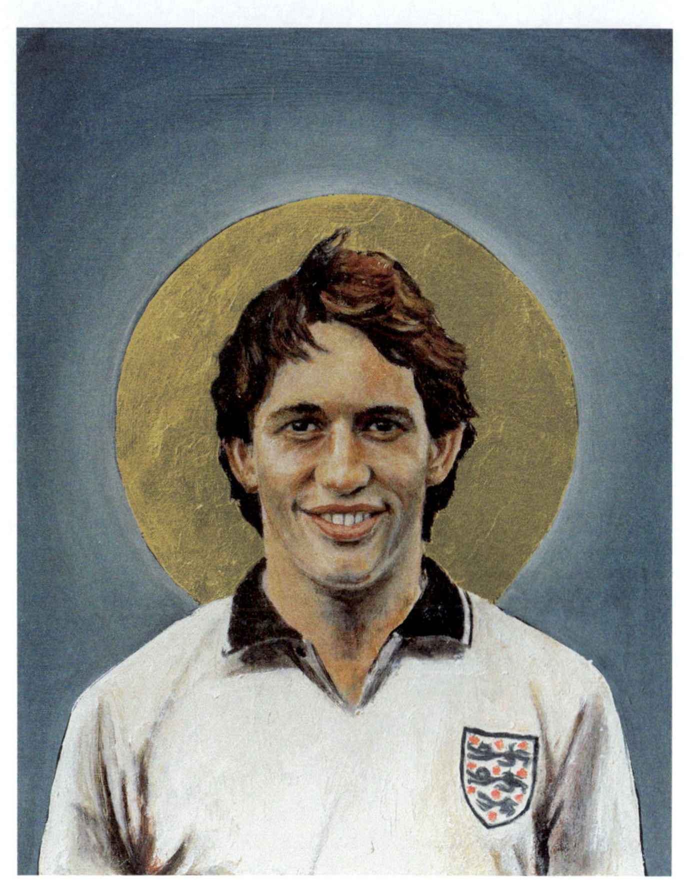

Gary Lineker

'If you won't stay, you don't play,' said the coach. So the team has to slog away without their best player till they're on their last legs. Only then does the tall blond get up from the bench, take off his tracksuit and say, 'I'm going to play now.' Three minutes later, the ball flies into the top corner. The tall blond had crept forward from deep in midfield and scored. His last shot in his very last match means the cup. The coach was still grumpy all the same.

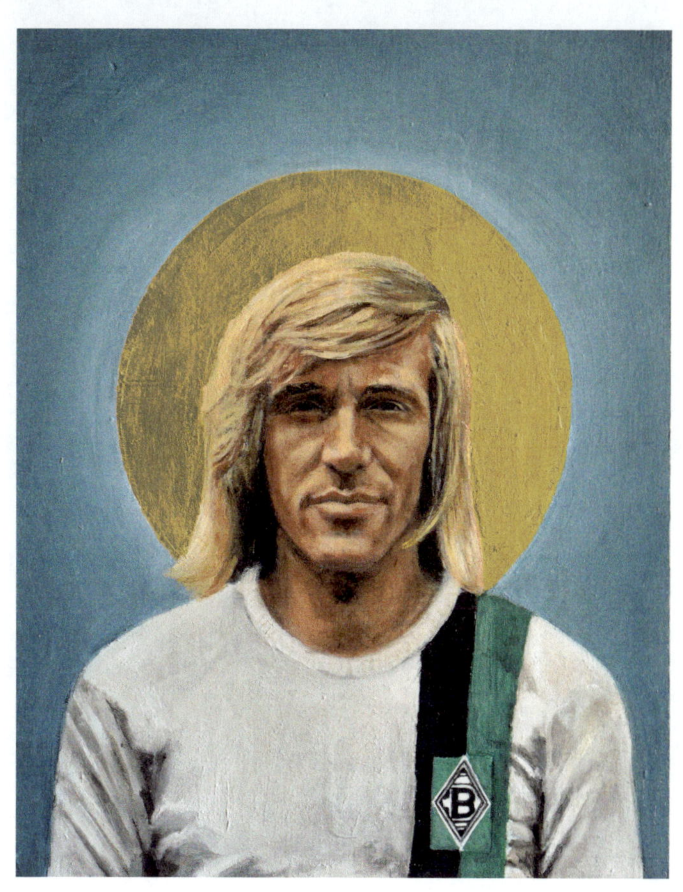

Günther Netzer

A certain resignation set in. Sure, the broadest and tallest defenders could form a wall. Sure, the goalie could have them close ranks to seal up even the slightest chink. But it was all in vain. Whenever he took a free kick, the fans would start to cheer even before the ball hit the net behind the motionless keeper.

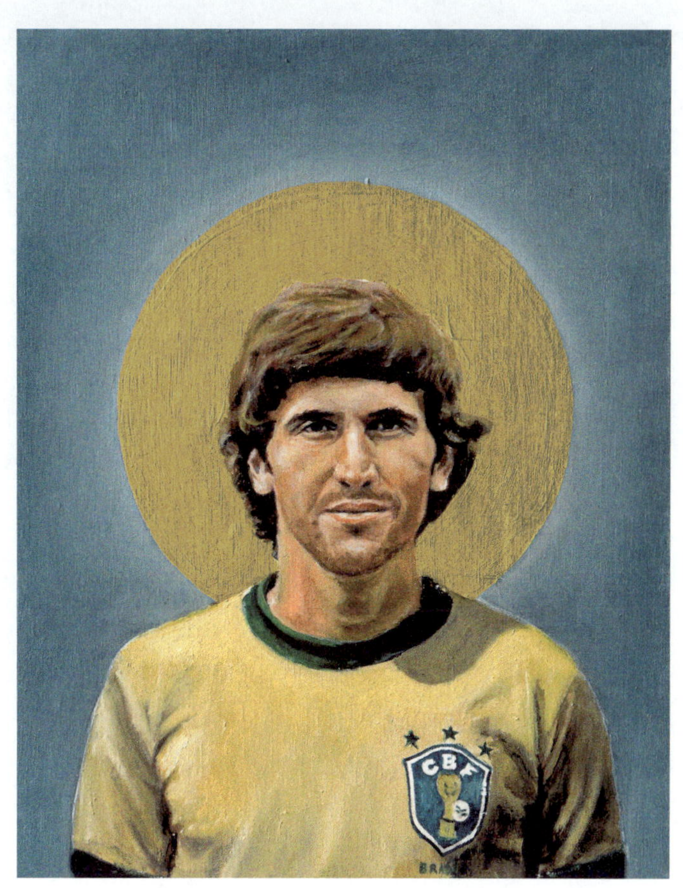

Zico

'Why does he look so sad?' the spectators wonder. 'He can outplay anyone!' But maybe the rumours are true after all: that he made a pact with the devil himself to become a peerless player, albeit one who'd never win any big trophies in this lifetime. So now he shines brightly down there on the pitch—with a look of deep sorrow on his face.

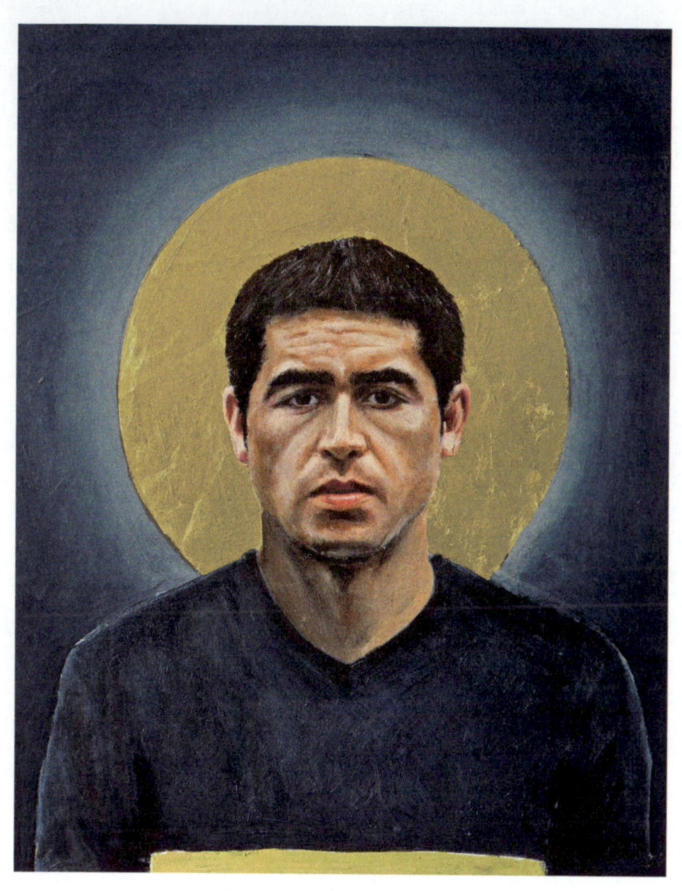

Juan Román Riquelme

He didn't even like football. He only played for the thrill of competition and for a handful of pesos. When he strode onto the pitch in his ghoulish black and white face paint, frightened kids would hide behind their parents. 'You paint your face, you go to war and you kill your rivals,' he said. After falling out with one coach after another, he'd have to hightail it off to the next club. Until a knee eventually gave out and he couldn't afford surgery to fix it. The life of this 'heavy-metal maestro' was cut short on the streets of Buenos Aires after two shots were fired—not by an opponent but by a robber.

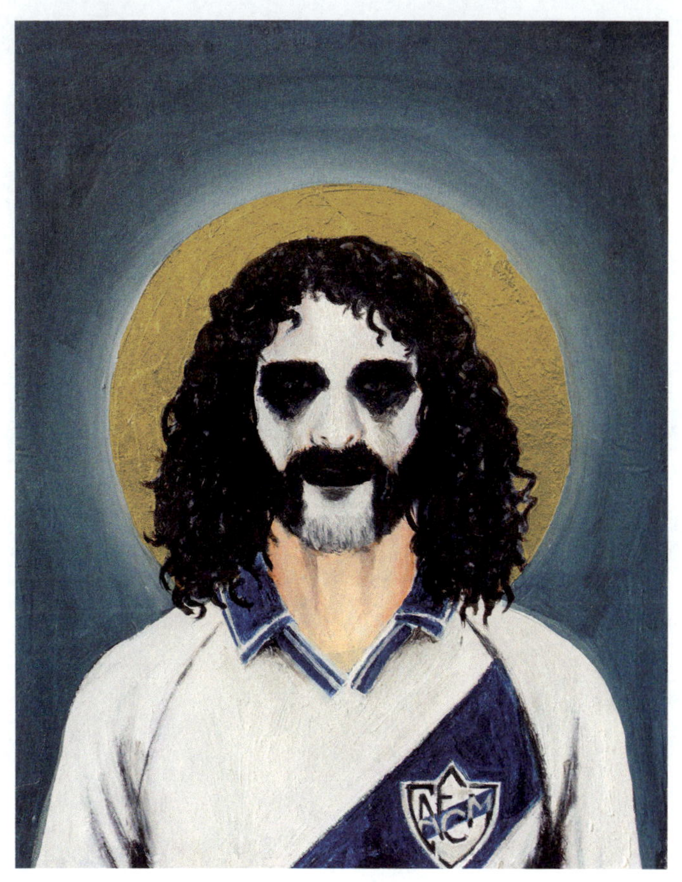

Darío Dubois

He knows nothing of modesty, humility or self-doubt. And why should he? What with his uncanny ability to promenade effortlessly through the backlines, win aerial duels with fakes and feints, bounce opponents off his broad chest like ping-pong balls, aim more accurately—even at long-range with a bicycle kick—than other strikers shooting from a standing position, and wield words as sharply as blades, he has no need to stop and think.

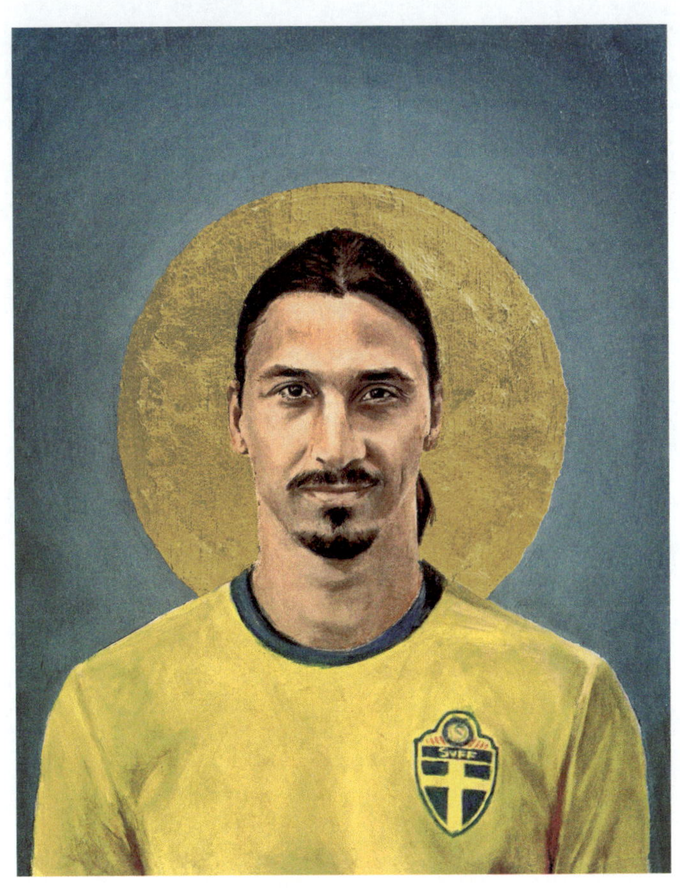

Zlatan Ibrahimović

'O say, can you see, by the dawn's early light…' And she takes a knee! The tidal wave of indignation that washes over her can't knock her down. Her super-human strength gives protection to the weak. The mightiest statues could be erected in her honour and they still wouldn't come close to reflecting her true stature.

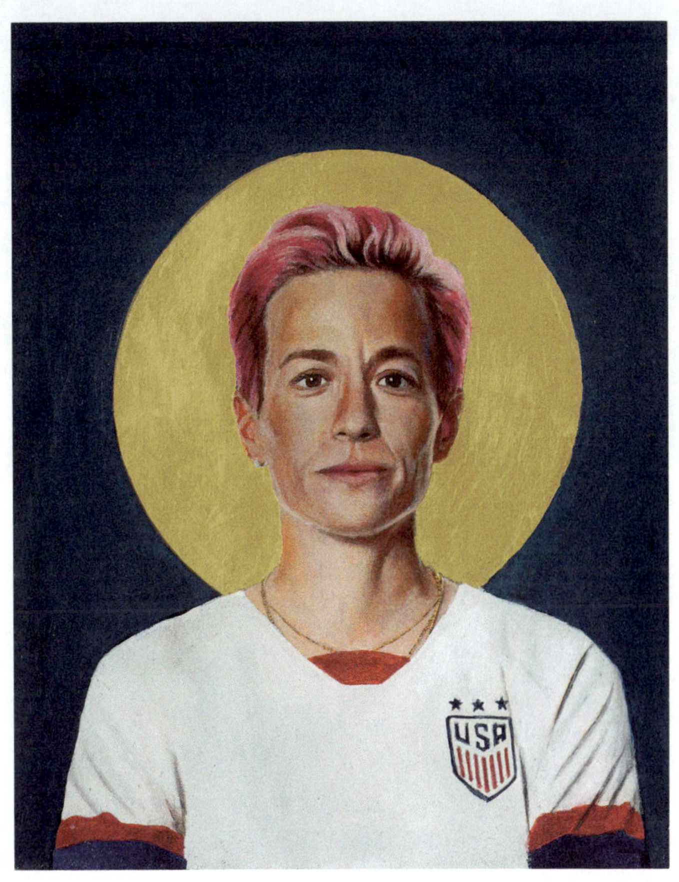

Megan Rapinoe

Had it not been for that one momentous feat, he'd have been just another name on the long list of those who joined the club from somewhere or other and then moved on to somewhere else, remembered only by a handful of aficionados. But in the ninety-third minute of the last match of the season, playing on the arch-rivals' turf, this centre back, who knows the opponent's goal only from afar, suddenly surges out in front and scores the title-winning goal. To this day, supporters in Zürich still praise his name to the skies.

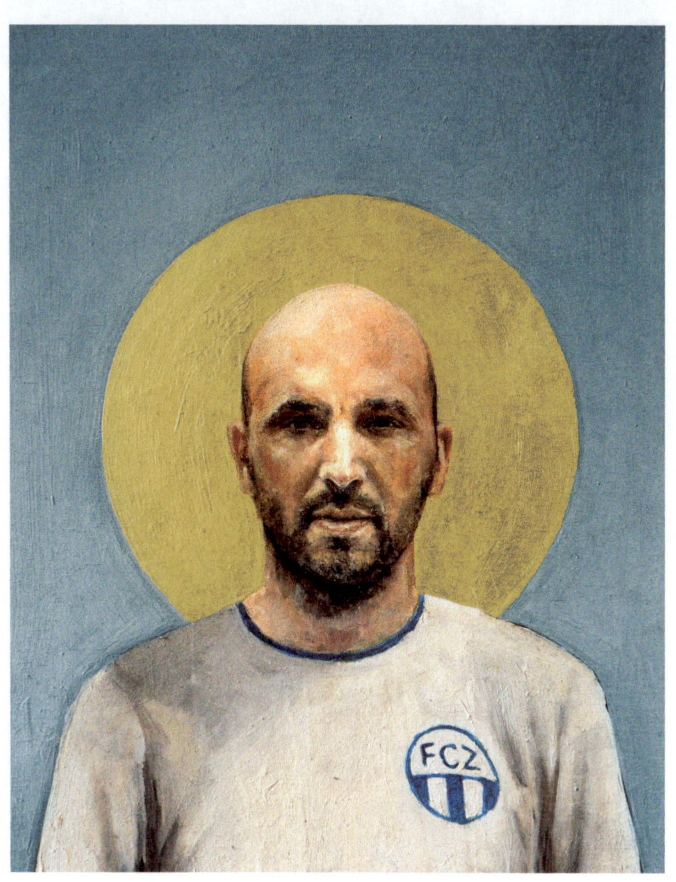

Iulian Filipescu

There are an infinite number of ways men can move about on the pitch. You'd need all the world's super-computers working in tandem to calculate all the possibilities and pinpoint the most promising one at any given moment in the state of play. But all he needs is a glance. And in a blink of an eye, defying all the laws of physics, his pass finds a friend, who, much to the latter's own astonishment, converts it.

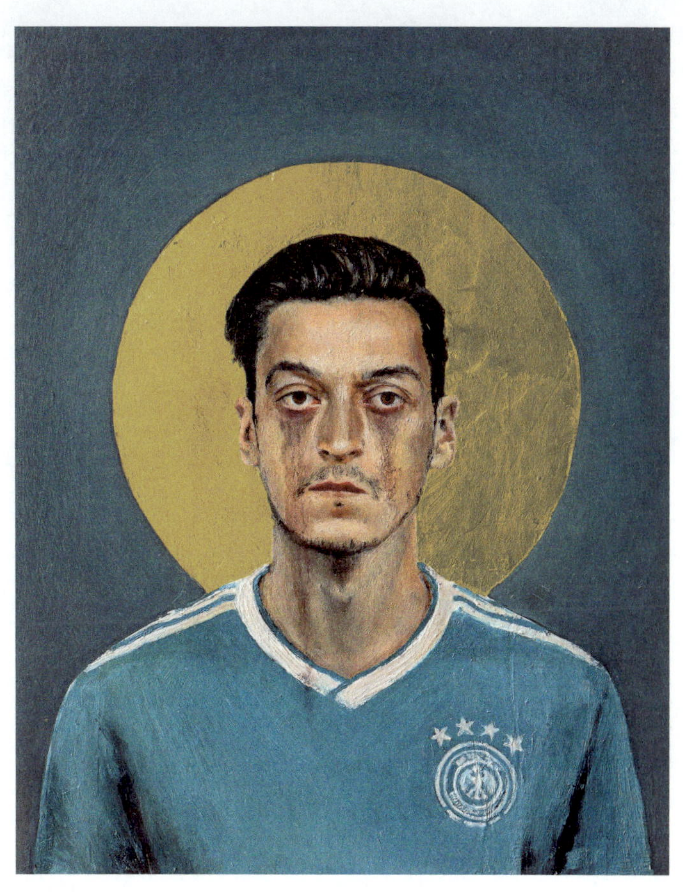

Mesut Özil

Index of Paintings

Part I

Part II

211	Daniele de Rossi	Commissioned	2019
215	Andrés Iniesta	On spec	2018
219	Steven Gerrard	Commissioned	2016
223	Thierry Henry	Commissioned	2016
227	Éric Cantona	Commissioned	2015
231	Hugo Sánchez	Commissioned	2016
235	Diego Simeone	On spec	2016
239	George Weah	Commissioned	2015
243	Gary Lineker	Commissioned	2017
247	Günther Netzer	Commissioned	2014
251	Zico	Commissioned	2014
255	Juan Román Riquelme	On spec	2018
259	Darío Dubois	On spec	2019
263	Zlatan Ibrahimović	Commissioned	2016
267	Megan Rapinoe	Commissioned	2020
271	Iulian Filipescu	Commissioned	2013
275	Mesut Özil	On spec	2018

All icons painted in oil and gold leaf on pine panel,
28×35 cm

The Authors

David Diehl (b. 1976)
is a Zürich-based multimedia artist and illustrator
who produces (often extensive) conceptual series
that may be topically or thematically open-ended or,
if commissioned by publishers or editors, narrowly
circumscribed. Over the past twenty years, much of
his work has been about religion as an aesthetic, the-
oretical and societal counterpart to artistic endeav-
our. Diehl is a hell of a footballer, in his dreams—just
like 'football's pre-eminent man of letters', the late,
great Eduardo Galeano.

Mämä Sykora (b. 1975)
is a journalist and the editor-in-chief of the Swiss
football magazine *Zwölf*. He also writes freelance
and co-hosts the football podcast *Sykora Gisler*. His
football career got no further, alas, than playmaking
in Zürich's alternative amateur league. Which is one
reason he's always had a weakness for brilliant but
sloppy players, who are having an increasingly hard
time of it in present-day football.

Andrés David Montenegro
Rosero (b. 1984)
was born and raised in the Colombian Andes and
is currently based in New England. He teaches contemporary, Latin American and pre-Columbian art as
well as museum studies. He's currently working on a

book to be titled *An Art History of Sports*. Montenegro Rosero has an ever-expanding collection of FC Barcelona memorabilia as well as a whole closetful of goalie jerseys—goalkeeper's his favorite position.

Alessandro Tione (b. 1998)
is a freelance photographer and content creator from Naples. He is the mastermind behind *Religione Monoteistica*, a photo project launched in 2018 to document Neapolitans' eternal veneration for Diego Maradona. He also writes and produces content for *Escape Vision*, a webzine about urban culture in Naples.

Asif Kapadia (b. 1972)
is a British multi-award-winning filmmaker known for his visually powerful documentaries based on archival footage. After winning the 2016 Oscar for Best Documentary Feature—and the hearts of Amy Winehouse fans—with *Amy*, the second film in his trilogy about 'child geniuses and fame', Kapadia won the hearts of football fans the world over with his third and last homage, *Diego Maradona*.

Image rights

Despite our best efforts, we have not been able to succeed in obtaining the copyrights and printing rights for all the photographs. Copyright holders are kindly asked to substantiate their claims, and recompense will be made according to standard practice.

David Diehl
ICONS

Texts   David Diehl, Mämä Sykora,
               Andrés David Montenegro Rosero
Translation   Eric Rosencrantz
Proofreading   Jacob Blandy

Book design   Studio Krispin Heé
               (Krispin Heé, Tim Wetter)
Printing   DZA Druckerei zu Altenburg GmbH
Paper   Iona Opak 60gm^2 (Planopak)
Font   ABC Social Extended

First edition Edition Patrick Frey, 2024
Print run   1200 copies
ISBN   ISBN 978-3-907236-70-3

Many thanks to Patrick Frey, Andreas Koller,
Tim Frey, Andrea Kempter, Asif Kapadia,
Zwölf magazine, all clients of the original icons,
Stefan Hell, Lisa Frauenfelder, Fernando,
Vasco and Nouria Frauenfelder.

Edition Patrick Frey
Schlossgasse 5
8003 Zürich, CH
www.editionpatrickfrey.com

Distribution

Switzerland:
AVA Verlagsauslieferung
Affoltern am Albis, CH
ava.ch

Germany, Austria:
GVA Gemeinsame
Verlagsauslieferung
Göttingen, DE
gva-verlage.de

France, Luxembourg,
Belgium:
Les presses du réel
Dijon, FR
lespressesdureel.com

United Kingdom:
Antenne Books
London, GB
antennebooks.com

United States:
ARTBOOK/D.A.P.
New York, US
artbook.com

Japan:
twelvebooks
Tokyo, JP
twelve-books.com

South Korea:
Post Poetics Co. Ltd.,
KR–Seoul
postpoetics.kr

Australia, New Zealand:
Perimeter Distribution
Melbourne, AU
perimeterdistribution.com

Other countries:
Edition Patrick Frey
Zürich, CH
editionpatrickfrey.com

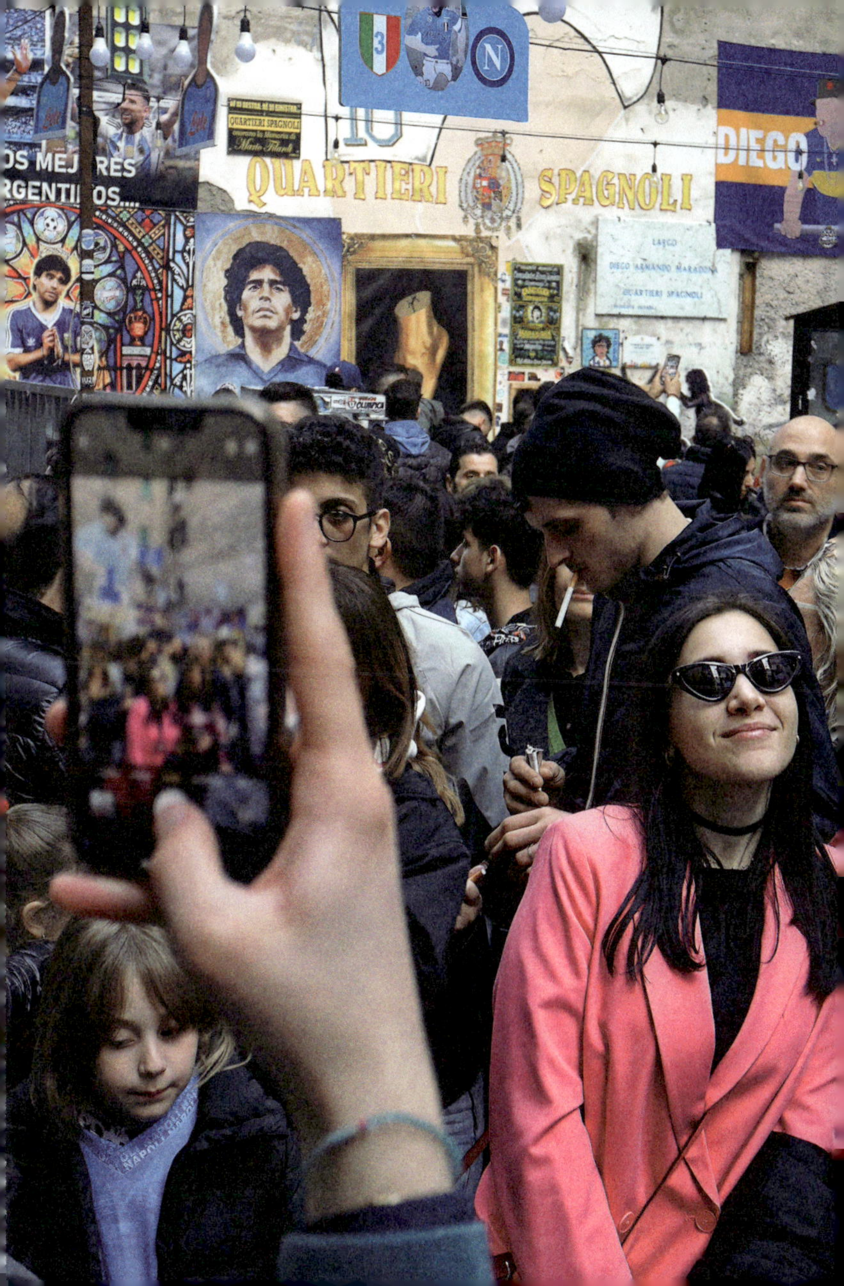

QUARTIERI SPAGNOLI
DIEGO
QUARTIERI SPAGNOLI
in memoria di
Mario Filardi
10
N
3
LARGO
DIEGO ARMANDO MARADONA
QUARTIERI SPAGNOLI
LOS MEJORES
ARGENTINOS...

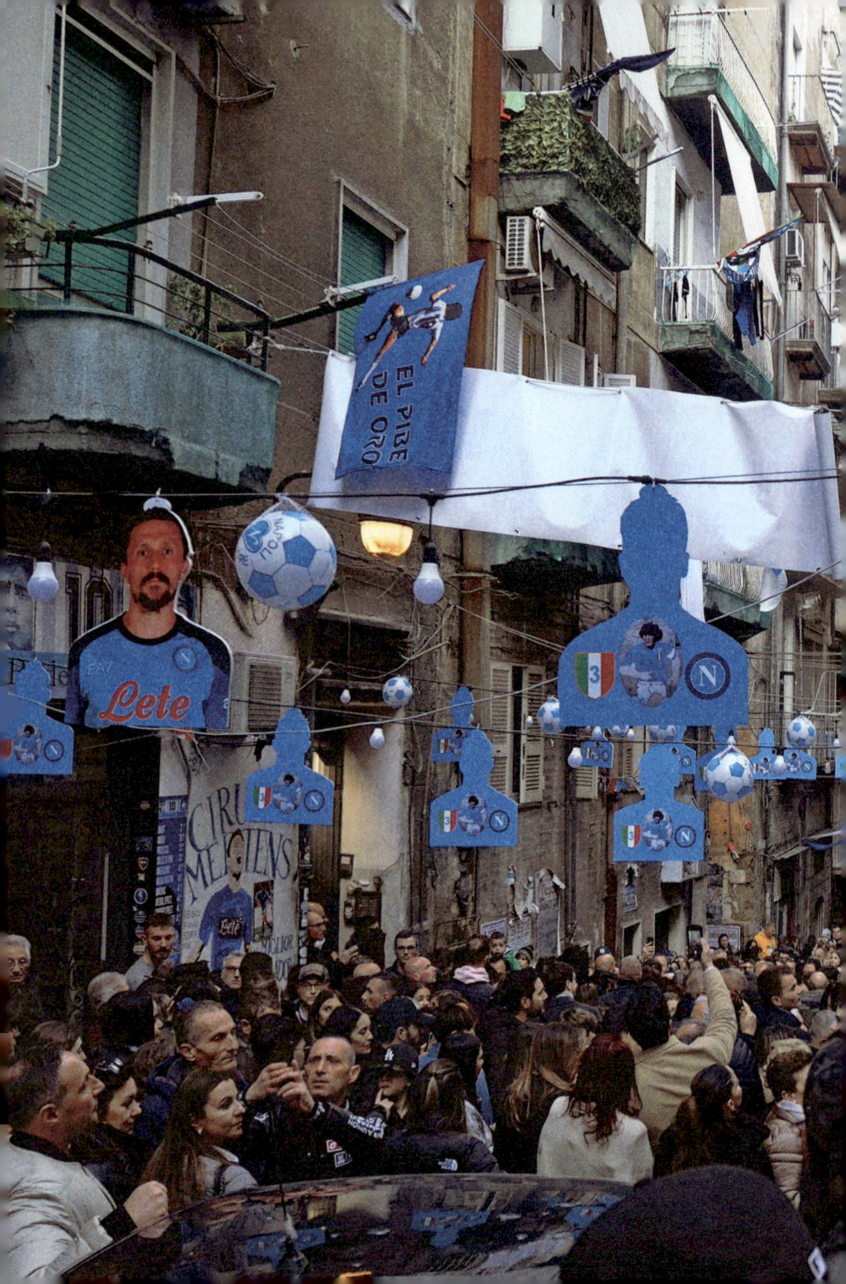

EL PIBE DE ORO
NAPOLI
Lete
CIRU
MERTENS
Lete